HIDDEN
HISTORY
of
OLD
TOWN

HIDDEN HISTORY

HISTORY

of

OLD

TOWN

Shirley Baugher

Charleston · London

THE
History
PRESS

Published by The History Press
Charleston, SC 29403
www.historypress.net

Cover painting: *Steve's Secret House* by Norman Baugher. Oil on canvas, 48 x 60 inches, 2011. *Visit saybaugher.com.*

First published 2011

Manufactured in the United States

ISBN 978.1.60949.207.6

Library of Congress Cataloging-in-Publication Data

Baugher, Shirley.
Hidden history of Old Town / Shirley Baugher.
p. cm.
Includes
ISBN 978-1-60949-207-6
1. Old Town (Chicago, Ill.)--History. 2. Old Town (Chicago, Ill.)--Biography. 3. Old Town (Chicago, Ill.)--Social life and customs. 4. Chicago (Ill.)--History 5. Chicago (Ill.)--Biography. 6. Chicago (Ill.)--Social life and customs. I. Title.
F548.68.O4B385 2011
977.3'11--dc23
2011017166

For Alex
Always an Old Towner

"Did you see anything?" they asked.
"Yes, wonderful things."

—Howard Carter, 1922, on making a tiny breach in the doorway leading to the inner chamber of Tutankhamen's tomb

CONTENTS

Friends Forever. Four Old Town boys, circa 1871. *Artist unknown.*

PREFACE

People tend to forget that the word "history" contains the word "story."
—Ken Burns

I am a storyteller with a tale to tell about Old Town—a Chicago neighborhood as old as the city itself and as new as tomorrow's headline; a neighborhood that has redefined itself with each passing age, fitting milestones and experiences, piece by piece, into the jigsaw puzzle of its history; a neighborhood of ordinary and extraordinary people who created an enclave of charm and civility in a boisterous and often unruly city; a magical little neighborhood that was, is and will be forever Old Town.

ACKNOWLEDGEMENTS

I am deeply grateful to all my Old Town neighbors and friends who made this book possible and especially to my husband, Norman—my infallible eye and the world's best graphic designer. Special thanks to Juliet, Carmela, Christine, Martha and Anthony Rago for the information on Henry Rago and to Linda Bensinger Olin for her invaluable social history of Crilly Court in the 1960s.

THE HIDDEN HISTORY TOUR BEGINS

History, with its flickering lamp, stumbles along the trail of the past, trying to reconstruct its scenes, to revive its echoes, and kindle with pale gleams the passion of former days.
—Winston Churchill

A LITTLE ABOUT OLD TOWN

Where and what is Old Town? And why should it interest you, the reader, enough to want to read an entire (hidden) history about it? Allow me to whet your appetite.

Old Town is, first and foremost, a neighborhood. In the grand scheme of things, it is not a famous, or even an infamous, neighborhood. Abe Lincoln did not sleep here, but he gave his name to the former resting place of many of our first settlers. We have no single residence that approaches the architectural triumph of the Glessner House, Henry H. Richardson's urban residential masterpiece at 1800 South Prairie Avenue (1885–87), or even the Henry B. Clarke House, constructed for the ages by an unknown architect at 1855 South Indiana Avenue (1836). Still, the five Louis Sullivan row houses on Lincoln Park West (1884), among the last of the famed architect's residential structures, remain as a testament to his greatness, and the John Boland House at 221 West Eugenie (1884) and St. Michael's Church (1872) have stood the test of time.

Louis Sullivan row houses, one of the famed architect's last remaining residential structures at 1834 North Lincoln Park West. *Photo by Carolyn Blackmon.*

A lot of (hidden) history lurks in Old Town. It's true, no president, Nobel Prize winner or *Time* magazine Person of the Year was born here. No notorious mobster was shot here. (Yes, John Dillinger was gunned down as he exited the old Biograph Theater a few blocks north on Lincoln Avenue, but it didn't actually happen in Old Town.) And Carl Sandburg was not thinking of quaint little Old Town when he dubbed the city "hog butcher for the world."

On the other hand, a renowned Lincoln scholar and director of the Chicago Historical Society (Paul Angle) lived in one of the area's last surviving farmhouses on Lincoln Park West. Some internationally acclaimed artists dipped brushes onto palettes in Old Town: Haddon Sunbloom created the Coca Cola Santa, Aunt Jemima and the Quaker Oats Man in his Crilly Court apartment. Ivan Albright conceived some of his macabre

A street in Old Town, 1940s. *Watercolor by Francis Chapin, from the collection of his daughter, Christine Chapin Harris.*

paintings, including the *Picture of Dorian Gray*, in a cluttered studio on the aptly designated "ghost of Ogden Avenue." And famed watercolorist Francis Chapin painted memorable city scenes, not on Chicago street corners or under the els, but on little Menomonee Street.

At least two prominent journalists got their start in Old Town: Bill Mauldin, who created the lovable "GI Joe dogfaces" of World War II and whose grieving Lincoln will be forever etched into our collective memories, and the quintessential Chicago journalist Herman Kogan, editor for the old *Chicago Sun Times* and author of the definitive book on Marshall Field's Department Store, for which he created the memorable tag line "Give the Lady What She Wants." A beloved children's poet, Eugene Field, sat overlooking Lincoln Park when he penned the line "The little toy dog is covered with dust, but sturdy and staunch he stands." And more than a few shady "favors" were done for friends in the DeLuxe Gardens, a now-defunct saloon on North Avenue owned by colorful Forty-third Ward alderman Paddy Bauler ("Chicago ain't ready for reform").

A lot of (hidden) history.

WHO ARE YOU, WHO WHO, WHO WHO?

Old Town is its own town within the city. On warm summer days, you can hear the sounds of children playing, dogs barking and neighbors chatting. Winter and summer, the bells of St. Michael's bind together the fragments of people and time into an orderly pattern of days. Old friendships endure and new relationships are formed. Famous names, outstanding citizens, everyday workers and people of every race, creed and color contribute to the melting pot that is Old Town. Christopher Porterfield, a *Time* magazine correspondent who lived in Old Town in the 1960s, captured the essence of the neighborhood when he wrote:

> *Old Town is a community in the sense that the common thread of its varied life, the principle of unity in all its diversity, is a kind of shared experience and shared outlook on life that reminds me of a small town, except that it's interwoven with so much that is cosmopolitan and sophisticated in Chicago.*

New York has Greenwich Village, New Orleans has its French Quarter, Paris has Montmartre and Chicago has its own little piece of charm that rivals all of them. Chicago has Old Town—an oasis in the steel and stone heart of the city, an old-fashioned, do-it-yourself family neighborhood.

The name Old Town was coined in recent years for the area bounded by the ghost of old Ogden Avenue on the west, North Avenue on the south and Clark Street on the east. It was once a community of German farmers affectionately dubbed "the Cabbage Patch." But that identification is long gone.

Today, Old Town is one of the city's most interesting neighborhoods—an interesting mix of nationalities, economic levels and rugged individualism. It is a melting pot (a potluck dinner once featured dishes of twenty-eight nationalities); an art colony (scores of well-known artists, writers and musicians lived here); a garden spot (famous in summer for its flowering patios, sundecks and window boxes); and a family village where a retired coal miner joins a renowned children's book author to share a gardening prize at the local art fair. Old Town is a small-town retreat from the city's furor, where people can work and live as they please and where almost no one cares whether skirts are long or short in any given year. It is a place where people with both dreams and dollars share a common bond of pride in their homes and their community.

Old Town is the embodiment of the "I Will" spirit of Chicago. It represents the determination of people in a community to make Chicago, in microcosm, a better place to live. Old Town is old settlers, a few famous names, outstanding citizens, and ordinary people—all with the same rights and all with the privilege of being something meaningful for the city dweller.

Hey, Good Looking: Old Town Architecture

I am always filled with happiness upon reaching home. Every rickety old house looks familiar—every tree an old friend. I was born here and have lived here and can never do ought but love our dear ugly Cairo.
—Isabella Maud Rittenhouse, 1881

One does not have to imagine how Old Town looked one hundred years ago. Walking its streets, a stroller comes face to face with history. Architect Seymour Goldstein described Old Town as a conglomeration of the "anonymous-builder's architecture"—referring to men in the building trades in the late 1800s and early 1900s who were often more adept and conscientious than professional architects. As a result of their skill and dedication, Old Town displays an elegance that defies time.

The look of Old Town fascinates residents and visitors alike. Buildings in the Old Town Triangle (a landmark district bounded by Clark Street, North Avenue and the aforementioned ghost of old Ogden Avenue) display a glorious mixture of styles—now termed Victorian—combining French, Italian Renaissance, Gothic and American immigrant.

One of the first things that strikes visitors about Old Town houses is their common scale and proximity to one another. They are about the same height and are packed so closely together that they seem to be dancing cheek to cheek. Lots are small and lawns are miniscule; nonetheless, ingenious Old Town gardeners have learned to create tiny Versailles on almost no land.

Old Town architecture is distinctive. Houses are wood or brick with some combinations of stone, ironwork and stucco. The frame buildings are recognizably nineteenth century—built between 1871 and 1874. (Three years after the Great Chicago Fire of 1871, frame construction was forbidden within the city limits, but more about that later.) They were built using a "balloon-frame method" that consisted of fastening two-by-four wall studs and two-by-twelve floor joists. This building method, which was

This page and next: Architectural details of historically significant Old Town houses: the famous "Angel Door" House; detail from a Louis Sullivan row house; detail from Old Town's only "mansion," the Frederick Wacker House; and floral motif and filigree railing from the Charles Wacker House. *Photos by Carolyn Blackmon.*

both easy and inexpensive, was so popular that it came to be known as the "Chicago Style." It was not until 1874 that three-story brick houses made their appearance.

Both the frame and brick structures were constructed by masons and carpenters who took pride in their work. They created finely wrought balustrades on the porches, carved ornate wooden doors, placed ornamental lintels over the windows, inserted handsome brackets along the roof lines and built interesting cornices and roof structures. It is fun to discover these houses—from an overall impression of materials and color seen from a distance to an appreciation of the elegant, sophisticated details realized close-up.

In the early twentieth century, low-rise brick apartment buildings (usually no more than four or five stories) made their appearance in Old Town. They had none of the distinctive features of the Victorian period and added little or nothing to the charm of the neighborhood. Fortunately, there are not very many of these.

Old Town's city plan can best be termed disorderly but charming. (It's hard to avoid the word "charming" when describing this neighborhood.) In a time when everything is built according to standards—proper street widths; proper setbacks; proper front, rear and side yards—Old Town functions very well with streets and lots of all widths and sizes. The streets are short—they start and stop and seem to go nowhere. It is difficult to park and impossible to speed under these conditions. Residents wouldn't have it any other way.

Well, enough introduction. It's time to take a walk through Old Town's hidden history, experience its character, take in its timeless beauty and absorb its atmosphere. Meet some of the neighbors who live and have lived here, share some of the events that have defined the community, listen to the chimes of St. Michael's and become, for a little while, an Old Towner. You'll be glad you did.

1

THE STORY BEGINS, WAY UP YONDER IN THE CABBAGE PATCH

And how fascinating history is—the long variegated pageant of man's still continuing evolution of this strange planet, so much the most interesting of all the myriads of spinners through space.
—George Macaulay Trevelyan

To begin my life at the beginning of my life, I was born.
—Charles Dickens

Those of us who are living in Old Town at the beginning of the twenty-first century play a unique role in its history. We can look back on all that it was and can look forward to what it may become. We know we are connected to a long line of strong, hardworking people who migrated here, built their homes here and lived their lives here. Some took permanent rest here; others moved on.

For the most part, we are not like those New England towns where family names remain the same for generations. We have been more transient. Consider the little house at 314 West Menomonee, where we begin and end our story. In the beginning, there was the Waldo family, who were the first occupants when the house was rebuilt after the Great Fire of 1871. The Waldos moved out, and the Lowensteins moved in. The Lowensteins left, and the Trues took over the house—only to be displaced by the Hansens. The Hansens gave way to the Ostroms; the Ostroms to the Altshuls; and the Altshuls to the Kees. After the Kees, the Cosmopolitan Bank assumed the mortgage for the house and later sold it to the Cashions, who in turn sold it to the O'Callahans. And, finally, the O'Callahans turned it over to the Weiss family. The names and the occupants are different, but they are all connected through their love and appreciation for that old house and this Old Town. All, especially the last owner, were united in a desire to preserve a remembrance of things past. That we know as much as we do about the house and about the community is a testament to their success.

A long time ago, when Chicago was very young (1833), what we now call Old Town was an uninhabitable, muddy marshland north of the business district crossed by a ten-mile ditch that carried floodwaters from Evanston to the Chicago River. In 1840, a series of democratic revolutionary movements broke out in many southern German towns and villages. Most of them were put down by force, causing thousands of oppressed people to leave Germany for America, hoping to find absolute political and religious freedom,

Map of Chicago in the 1830s. Chicago Tribune, *January 30, 1983.*

economic advancement and, in general, a better life—much as the Pilgrims and Puritans had done two hundred years earlier.

The people who came were not destitute farmers or poor artisans. They were working-class individuals who couldn't support their families when estates were broken up or divided among all the sons. They were, for the most part, a diverse people who wanted no restrictions on the development of society and free expression of their political ideas: Catholics, Masons, carpenters, laborers and farmers.

Chicago was not their first destination. They went to New York and then Pennsylvania. They came to Chicago at the request of the Redemptorist fathers and in the hope of jobs and cheap land. Most of all, they were attracted to the city's vigorous and supportive Catholic Church. They settled in the area west of Clark Street, near factories on the Chicago River. In a short period of time, they had created those institutions that characterize a community: churches, medical facilities, fraternal organizations and schools. In 1846, they built St. Joseph's Church at Chicago and Wabash Avenues, and they were content—for a while. But by 1851, the marshland to the north had dried up, and the land became habitable, prompting municipal officials to extend the city limits to what is now Fullerton Avenue.

The lure of free or cheap land was irresistible. In the pioneering spirit of the nineteenth century, some German settlers moved to the meadows above North Avenue. They converted the dried-up swampland into cow pastures and truck gardens for growing potatoes, cabbages and celery—but mostly cabbages. So many cabbages, in fact, that the farmers dubbed their little area "the Cabbage Patch." Some of what they grew was kept for home consumption; the rest was sold to satisfy the appetites of a growing urban population.

At first, the farmers commuted back and forth between their houses south of North Avenue and their fields to the north. Inevitably, they tired of commuting and started to build small, single-family cottages on their properties. The most common early building style was the balloon-frame cottage—so called because of the system used to frame a wooden building. All vertical structural elements of the exterior bearing walls and partitions consisted of single studs, which extended the full height of the frame, from the top of the soleplate to the roof plate. The four wall studs were two-by-four and the floor joists, two-by-twelve. The floor joists were fastened to the studs by machine-made nails. This kind of structure, which came to be known as "the Chicago Style," was ideal because the early Old Town houses were not designed by architects and

A one-and-a-half-story balloon-frame cottage at 217 West Eugenie Street, in the famous Chicago Style. *Photo by Carolyn Blackmon.*

put up by construction firms; rather, they were built by masons and tradesmen who could put together a balloon-frame cottage with a hammer, a saw, some nails and a couple of weeks' time. Best of all, the materials used to construct the cottages were readily available and inexpensive.

Most balloon-frame cottages were one and a half stories high—high enough to accommodate future street gradings—and were built on log or brick foundations. The first floor was used for storage. Steep stairs led to a second level, which contained the living quarters. A peaked roof topped the structure in front and back. The houses were surrounded by gardens and flower beds and had barns in the rear.

There was a second frame house style, larger than the cottage, that was also popular with early builders. Like the balloon-frame model, it had a

The Story Begins, Way Up Yonder in the Cabbage Patch

A two-story balloon-frame cottage at 229 West Eugenie, built in 1874, also in the Chicago Style. *Photo by Carolyn Blackmon.*

Frame cottages on Eugenie Street. *Oil painting by Norman Zimmerman.*

wood frame and was covered with clapboard siding or shingles. Tall and narrow, this structure consisted of two or two and a half stories and looked a little like a farmhouse, with slightly overhanging wooden eaves and simple wood trim. Both styles filled the streets of Old Town until 1871, when the Great Fire destroyed them all (see page 56).

You might have thought that residents would choose to move outside the city limits after the fire. They did not. In fact, residents rebuilt new frame cottages on the ashes of burned-out homes. The Chicago Relief and Aid Society made this possible by selling inexpensive house plans and "kits" to those who had been made homeless. They offered two different-sized cottages, each consisting of two rooms (actually one large room and a divider) and both employing balloon-frame construction. One plan, measuring

The ladies of West Eugenie, three Chicago-style cottages in the 200 block of West Eugenie, built shortly after the Great Chicago Fire of 1871. *Photo by Carolyn Blackmon.*

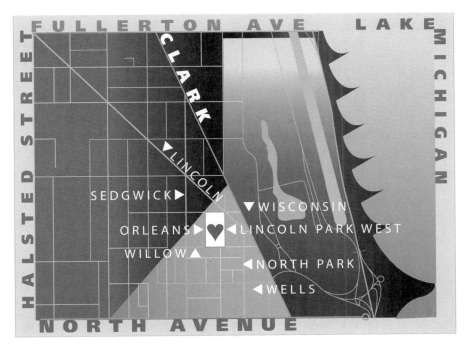

Old Town map. *Courtesy of Norman Baugher.*

twelve by sixteen feet, was meant for families of three. The second plan, measuring twenty by sixteen feet, was intended for families of more than three. The plan came complete with lumber framing and boards, felt lining for the inside walls, a double iron chimney, two (four-paneled) doors, three windows and a partition that could be placed wherever the occupants chose. The houses were built at a central city location and then moved by wagon to burned-out lots. More than fifty-two hundred of these cottages were constructed, at a cost of $75 (for the smaller kit) or $100 (for the larger kit). In 1874, the city passed an ordinance banning the construction of wooden residences within the city limits. But between 1871 and 1874, entire blocks of these houses went up in Old Town, and they can still be seen today.

With the new houses came demographic changes. Although Germans continued to dominate the area, eastern Europeans, Irish, Italians and French moved in and enriched the Cabbage Patch, as well as the city, with their talents. They were shoemakers, tailors, brewers, carpenters, railroad workers and grain elevator operators. They brought in a new era of growth and change, including the name of their community. With the new century, the Cabbage Patch became North Town.

2

GIVE ME THAT OLD-TIME RELIGION

A Tale of Two Churches

History is like an open Bible; historians are not priests to expound it infallibly; [their] function is to teach people to read it and reflect upon it for themselves.
—*George Macaulay Trevelyan*

WE GATHER TOGETHER: ST. MICHAEL'S CHURCH AND THE GERMAN CATHOLIC PEOPLE OF OLD TOWN

Religion was very important to the German community in the Midwest. Until 1850, Cabbage Patch parishioners worshipped at St. Joseph's Catholic Church at Chicago and Wabash Avenues. As the north side population grew, however, residents decided they needed a neighborhood parish. In 1852, Michael Diversey, part owner of the Diversey and Lill Brewery and a prominent member of St. Joseph's, donated a plot of land at North and Hudson Avenues for a church. In four months, local builders completed a forty- by sixty-foot frame building and placed a single bell in the cupola. The finished building cost $730, money that was raised by the residents themselves. In appreciation of their benefactor's generosity, parishioners dedicated the new church to St. Michael, Mr. Diversey's patron saint. At that time, there were forty-three families in the congregation.

Michael Diversey owned other large tracts of land on Chicago's north side. These were annexed by the city in the 1850s, extending Chicago's northern border to what is now Fullerton Avenue. The availability of this property within the city limits attracted a number of prosperous and politically prominent citizens to the north side. William B. Ogden, Chicago's first mayor, moved into what is now the Gold Coast area in 1856—as did William Rand and Andrew McNally, who later gained fame as map publishers. Irish, Italian and French immigrants migrated to the Cabbage Patch—building their homes alongside those of the German residents—and added their talents to Chicago's workforce as shoemakers, tailors, brewers, carpenters, railroad workers and grain elevator operators.

Like the rest of the city, the Cabbage Patch was experiencing tremendous economic and social growth. Under Mayor Ogden's leadership, the first swing bridge was built over the Chicago River, allowing inhabitants to move more freely from one part of the city to another. Ogden promoted the building of miles of railroads, which enabled farmers to get their produce to other markets, as did the Illinois and Michigan Canal and the Chicago and Michigan Steam Boat Company. The razing of a red-light district just south of the Cabbage Patch made the area an even more desirable place to live and encouraged businessmen like Michael Diversey and William Lill to invest in the area. Their Lill and Diversey Brewery Company became the largest brewery west of New York, covering two city blocks and shipping more than forty thousand barrels of beer a year all over the nation. Unfortunately, the company burned to the ground in the Great Chicago Fire of 1871 and was never rebuilt.

A Church Grows in Old Town

Michael Diversey's legacy was not his enormously successful brewery, however; rather, it was St. Michael's Church. During the Civil War, Chicago became an important commercial center, supplying munitions and material for the war effort and food for the expanding population. The economic boom times attracted even more immigrants to the city and to St. Michael's Church. By 1862, the congregation had outgrown its tiny building and determined to replace it. A postwar depression did not discourage the priest and parishioners of St. Michael's from going ahead with their rebuilding plans. They even added several other needed facilities to the project. Enterprising parishioners obtained land at Cleveland and Eugenie Streets, the site of the current establishment, and raised money to build a much larger brick and stone structure with a school, a convent and a home for priests. They broke ground in September 1866. The priests' order, the Redemptorist fathers, literally went door-to-door begging for contributions. By November of that year, they had laid the cornerstone. Over the next three years, the work moved along. The exterior walls were constructed from red sandstone and locally made bricks and extended two hundred feet front to back. The two-hundred-foot-high steeple was taller than the Chicago Water Tower and was, for a while, one of the tallest structures in the city. In September 1869, the feast day of St. Michael, parishioners and local dignitaries gathered to dedicate the completed building. The new complex cost $130,000, 178 times as much as the original building.

Parishioners expected to be comfortably ensconced in their new church for a long, long time. But fate intervened on the night of October 8, 1871, when a fire that began in Mrs. O'Leary's barn on DeKoven Street spread north, destroying almost everything in its path. (There will be more about the fire in a separate chapter.) As the fire approached St. Michael's, the bells began to toll. Parishioners gathered outside the church, confident that their building, which was built of brick and stone, would stand. Their confidence faltered when they saw the Holy Name Cathedral, St. Joseph's Church and the Alexian Hospital go up in flames; they knew that St. Michael's would be next. Priests, brothers, nuns and parishioners began to remove the church's treasures—the large wooden crucifix, Bibles, candelabra, statues and altarpieces—which they buried in the monastery grounds. They loaded the hand-carved Stations of the Cross, vestments and altar cloths onto a wagon and sent them to safety at Rosehill, outside the city limits—just in the nick of time. The flames roared through all the parish buildings, destroying them. Only two walls of the church remained. The altar fixtures and the statues that were buried in the ground burned. Even the huge bells dropped from the tower and melted in the intense heat. Gone, too, were the school, the sisters' convent and the priests' home.

But the spirit of St. Michael's was not gone, not by any means. No sooner had the fire run its course than parishioners shoveled the ashes into the basement and began rebuilding. (In the 1970s, these ashes were discovered during an excavation under the church—a link to the Great Fire and a truly "hidden history.") As a temporary measure, neighbors propped a ninety-foot wooden shanty against a surviving stone wall in the church garden. Two weeks later, on October 22, priests conducted services in this makeshift shelter. When masses were not being said, the priests and brothers lived in the shanty, sleeping on burlap sacks filled with straw and balancing plates on their knees at mealtime.

By November 1871, local carpenters had erected another building, which was used as both a church and a school until damage to the main building was repaired (at a cost of $40,000). The new building was then used exclusively as a school. On October 12, 1872, one year after the fire, parishioners celebrated the completion of their renovated church. The next year, they held a big parade to commemorate St. Michael's "resurrection." Marching bands from parishes all over the city met at Erie Street and walked two miles north to the church. They stopped before a huge wreath inscribed with gold letters: "Welcome you friends from far and near; to bless this, the house of our Lord most dear." The bells were not hung until 1876. There were five of them cast in bronze by the McShane Company. They were named St. Michael, St. Mary, St. Joseph, St. Alphonsus and St. Theresa.

For the next several years after the fire, the priest at St. Michael's, Father De Dyeker, his staff and parishioners continued to rebuild. A boys' school was opened in 1873. In 1874, the Brothers of Mary, a teaching order, took over the operation of the school. The Poor Handmaids of Jesus Christ, a nursing order, joined the parish in 1874. The sisters taught the kindergarten children and took care of the sick who were homebound. In 1876, the rectory was completed at 1633 North Cleveland Avenue, along with a new convent for the teaching nuns. By February 1877, members had joined with Father De Dyeker to observe St. Michael's silver anniversary. It was a grand moment. From a tiny wooden church comprising forty families, the church had grown to be the largest German parish in the city, with a school that housed 1,527 children.

St. Michael's and Old Town entered the twentieth century together. They experienced the demographic changes and occupational diversity that came with the influx of eastern Europeans in the early part of the century. They enjoyed the thriving economy brought on by the industrial era. They saw their parishioners through the Depression and the hard times that hit the neighborhood as a result of foreclosures and rising unemployment. They were an enclave of stability during the turbulent 1950s and '60s, when gypsies and gangs took over the area. And they were a symbol of the hope and resilience that mark the future of the church and the community it serves.

The story of St. Michael's is well known among its parishioners and many other Chicagoans since it was by far the largest church in the Cabbage Patch and one of the largest in the city. But the neighborhood had other churches with stories that were less familiar. Here are two of them.

THE LITTLE CHURCH ON CLARK STREET

Many people walk past the little church at 1754 North Clark Street and never really see it. The truth is, it's not a destination for most people who live in Old Town. Its parishioners come from other neighborhoods, for the most part—although they have a long connection and commitment to this church and to its location. This is part of their history.

The Hermon Baptist Church has been at 1754 North Clark for well over one hundred years. Its story has some interesting parallels with the history of St. Michael's. By the late 1880s, the population of Old Town had become more heterogeneous. There were now Irish, Italians, Assyrians, Filipinos, Greeks and Japanese living among the Germans. Wealthy families from the

Hermon Baptist Church. The little brick church on Clark Street, home of the founding Senior Choir members. *Photo by Carolyn Blackmon.*

south and west sides of the city moved into the Gold Coast and Old Town areas and commissioned more elaborate houses of brick and stone. They employed a number of African Americans as domestics. Those who didn't have room for their servants in their Gold Coast residences often housed them in Old Town apartments.

The 1880s were difficult times for African Americans. Even in the North, the atmosphere was charged with the prejudices that prevailed in the aftermath of Reconstruction and the passage of Jim Crow laws. In his book, *Chicago: The Second City*, Joseph Liebling recounted the story of a white couple struggling with packages after a Christmas shopping expedition in the Loop in the 1940s. Though cabs were scarce, they waved on an African American taxi driver cruising on State Street—preferring to stand and wait in the bitter cold until a white driver came by. Mr. Liebling, a liberal New Yorker, gladly took the cab and asked the cabbie if he had rightly interpreted what just happened. The driver assured him that he had. "They passed me up because I'm colored," he said. "Many of them do."

There were not many people of color living on the near north side of Chicago; nor were there churches or meeting places where those who did live here could worship. Isolated in a white, middle-class enclave, thirteen domestics joined together in 1887 to form a singing club under the leadership of Mr. Jordan Allen. They called themselves the Senior Choir and became a nucleus of what was to become the Hermon Baptist Church.

The Senior Choir met at different houses each Sunday, often traveling to the far south side of Chicago to hold their meetings. Because they had to go by horse and buggy or walk, they arrived home very late on Sunday evenings or early on Monday mornings—sometimes barely in time to report for work. But faith prevailed over geography. They came together despite the hardships and looked for ways to improve their situation. Eventually, they got permission to meet in the basement of the LaSalle Street Baptist Church (an all-white institution) on Sunday afternoons, after the regular church members had completed their services.

Meeting at the LaSalle Street church was only a temporary solution, however, and not an ideal one. The problem of discrimination remained. The small congregation needed to be with others of its own faith and color. In its search for a Baptist congregation with which to merge, it found the Bethesda Baptist Church on South Dearborn Street—still a long commute but an improvement over their treatment by the white members of LaSalle

Street Baptist. The pastor of Bethesda, the Reverend Jordan Chavis, welcomed the thirteen domestics into his congregation.

Despite the acceptance by the members of Bethesda, the hardship of travel back and forth took its toll. Fortune finally smiled on the Senior Choir in the form of the Reverend J.F. Thomas, pastor of the Olivet Baptist Church. Together, Reverend Thomas and Reverend Chavis organized the thirteen into a church of their own—which they called the Hermon Baptist Church after Mount Hermon, a mountain outside Jerusalem. Hermon Baptist was first housed in the basement of Turner Hall on Clark Street, just south of Chicago Avenue. When Turner Hall was torn down to make way for the Chestnut Street Post Office, the group moved to a building on the corner of Franklin and Whiting (now Walton) Streets. They remained at this location until 1897, when they finally found a home of their own at 1754 North Clark Street.

And therein lies another story. Old Town is full of them. Prior to 1875, the property had been owned by Mr. and Mrs. Augusta Paulse. They deeded the land to a group known as the Chicago Society of the New Jerusalem. Mr. and Mrs. William M. Le Moyer increased the size of the property by donating an additional ten feet to the original plot, plus the area to the parkway line. The "angels" of Hermon Baptist took it from there. Sister Lucy Everage made the down payment on a building. Dr. Manning, a white trustee of the Baptist Association, joined Hermon Baptist and helped the congregation move into the church facility. This support was critical because, at the time, African Americans could not own property. With Dr. Manning on the board of trustees, the sale and ownership of the site could be finalized. On May 1, 1902, the trustees of the Chicago Society of the New Jerusalem officially deeded the land and property at 1754 North Clark Street to the Hermon Baptist Church.

Hermon Baptist has thrived in its present location. In 1925, the church was enlarged to accommodate a growing congregation. Its indebtedness was first reduced through a bond issue and later completely paid off. On Sunday, October 22, 1944, parishioners held a ceremony and burned the mortgage paper.

Eliminating the mortgage did not ensure happily ever after. Hermon has had to stave off real estate developers who wanted to buy the property and move the church to another location. When many members of the congregation moved from the north to the south side, the pastor provided bus transportation so that families could continue to worship at their church.

And even after a successful rebuilding effort, church staff has had to struggle to keep existing members and attract new ones.

Today, the membership has grown from the original 13 to 345. Of these, about 170 attend services on any given Sunday. There are 9 deacons to look after the spiritual needs and physical well being of parishioners. A group of associate ministers conducts monthly seminars on important issues. A Baptist training union works with prospective congregants to be inducted into church membership, and a host of support groups attend to ongoing needs. In addition to regular Sunday morning worship services, Hermon holds Sunday school, Bible study classes, choir rehearsals and programs by visiting churches.

You've heard the saying "The more things change, the more they stay the same." More than one hundred years ago, the thirteen Senior Choir founders traveled the length of the city to sing and worship together. Today, 345 members come from all over Chicagoland to sing and pray together: from Homewood, Bellwood, Maywood, Lynwood, South Holland and points north. The difference is, they don't have to ride in horse-drawn buggies or walk, and they get home before they have to go to work on Monday morning. Faith still transcends geography.

THE STORY OF MARIE BUTLER: ONE OF THE FAITHFUL

No one typified the Hermon spirit more than Marie Butler. Although Marie passed away a few years ago, she will never leave the church on Clark Street. She attended services there for more than sixty years and was a mainstay of the congregation. Marie was born and lived much of her life in a little house at 207 West Division Street. Her children grew up there and went to school in the neighborhood: Waller and Franklin. She spoke of a time, in the 1930s, when both sides of Wells Street, from Division to Menomonee, were primarily residential and said that many of the residents went to Hermon Baptist. She remembered Dr. Scholl's Shoe Factory, little grocery stores, a theater where her children saw movies for ten cents, a drugstore and a bakery. She shopped at a long-gone A&P Grocery Store on East Division where, she said, a lot of movie stars came to pick up food. The locals used to go there hoping to see someone famous.

Her house on Division Street was owned by a "kind and generous" Japanese gentleman named Mr. Asato, who had extensive commercial and

Marie Butler, one of the Hermon faithful for over sixty years. *Photo by Sally Butler.*

residential holdings in the area, including a grocery store, a laundromat and a currency exchange. Most of her family worked for Mr. Asato, and many students owed their educations to him. He would bring young people over from Japan to study in America and let them live in his own home.

Marie worked for years as a file clerk and a typist for the county—"No computers," she said, "just good, old-fashioned Remington typewriters." She had a strong work ethic, instilled by her family. She worked, her husband worked and her children worked. When she retired from her job as a file clerk, she took up sewing, attending classes at the old Fair Store on State Street. While she enjoyed sewing, she didn't always enjoy the people for whom she sewed. "They were very demanding," she said, "and they often wanted things that didn't become them," but she couldn't oppose them. So she stopped sewing for adults and started making clothes for Barbie dolls. The Barbies had no fashion demands or complaints.

Her children grew up and moved away. But Marie stayed in the house on Division Street, vowing never to leave. She did. Her brother, who had fought in World War II and won two Purple Hearts for bravery, returned home and bought a house on the west side. He wanted his sister and her husband to move in with him. Marie refused at first because she didn't want to go so far away from her church. She relented only because her neighborhood had changed. The Cabrini Green housing project and the influx of gangs brought crime and unrest to the north side. And so she left—but not really. Her spirit stayed.

3
THERE IS A TAVERN IN THE TOWN

The Saloons and Breweries of Old Town

*Faithfulness to the truth of history involves far more than research,
however patient and scrupulous, into special facts. Such facts may be
detailed with the most minute exactness, and yet the narrative, taken as
a whole, may be unmeaning or untrue. The narrator must seek to imbue
himself with the life and spirit of the time. He must study events in
their bearings near and remote; in the character, habits, and manners
of those who took part in them. He must be, as it were, a sharer or a
spectator of the action he describes.*
—*Francis Parkman*

Chicago has always been a great saloon city (about one saloon to every
sixty families). In the 1890s, about 500,000 Chicagoans used a saloon's
services on any given day. Old Town has had its share of popular taverns.
From the nineteenth century, when C.H. Nieman and Company served as
a combination feed store and saloon, through the twentieth and twenty-first
centuries, when the likes of Koenigsberg's, Zahners, DeLuxe Gardens, Twin
Anchors, Marge's, the Old Town Ale House, Corcorans, Wells on Wells
and many more catered to the thirsty. Along with the saloons, there were
breweries and brewmasters, who both lived and opened establishments in
the neighborhood. Here are a few of their stories.

A TAVERN IN OLD TOWN

There is a tavern in the town,
And there my true love sits him down
And drinks his wine as merry as can be
And never, never thinks of me.
—F.J. Adams, 1891

Old Town saloons have played a very important part in the neighborhood's history. The saloons were more than just places to buy a beer or a shot. They were community centers where neighbors got together and shared news and concerns. They were social clubs. They were places of refuge and recreation for hardworking residents. The barkeep or owner often served as an ear for family troubles, as well as a banker to lend money to patrons who were down on their luck and an employment service to hook up workers with potential employers. Saloons provided ethnic newspapers (usually German) for those who could not read English. Saloons served fast sandwiches to factory workers looking for a quick lunch during the noon break and filled lunch pails with beer. When a big room was needed for a wedding, anniversary, dance or labor meeting, salons provided it. On hot summer nights, many immigrants paid the saloonkeeper a nickel to sleep on the cool saloon floor. One English visitor, William Stead, in *If Christ Came to Chicago* (1894), said of the saloonkeepers that "they practiced the fundamental principle of human brotherhood which Christ came to teach."

A favorite Old Town neighborhood drinking establishment in the late nineteenth century was C.H. Nieman and Company. Built in the 1870s, it was a combination feed store and saloon—not unusual in those days. A large sign on the front of the building announced that it belonged to "C.H. Niemann and Company, Commission Merchant," selling "Flour, Feed and Country Produce." Farmers who drove their carts from agricultural areas north of Fullerton Avenue would arrive during the early morning and buy feed for their stock. Afterward, they would stop next door to discuss the news and take liquid refreshment.

Neiman's feed store/tavern was then sold to Mr. Charles Koenigsberg. "Charley" decided to gussy up the place. He added Victorian gingerbread features to the façade and changed the sign from C.H. Nieman to Charley's. As a further step up, he offered "Imported Wines and Cigars" and printed their availability on the window. The men traded their factory clothes for frock coats and top hats. Charley's was strictly a man's domain. Women were not allowed inside, although Mr. Koenigsberg and his family had an apartment above the

Klungel's Lager Beer Salon & Feed Store. *ICHI-06007. Photographer unknown.*

Charley's Wells Street Saloon. *ICHI-04870. Photographer unknown.*

establishment on the second floor. His children, Walter and Irma, were born there and chose to live in the neighborhood after the tavern was sold.

The old saloon gained a citywide following in 1908, after it was purchased by the Zahners, the most successful of all the owners. Zahners became a popular Chicago haunt for patrons who came to linger at its ornate bar. A special feature was an elegant ladies' café that allowed wives to come in and enjoy themselves while their husbands frequented the other side. Men drank their beer from carved steins imported from Europe and were entertained by a jangly mechanical piano. A huge portrait of Mayor Carter Harrison presided over the merriment.

But, as the saying goes, all good things must come to an end. So it was with Zahner's. The beautiful old building deteriorated with age and was not bought or renovated. It fell to the wrecker's ball in the early 1950s, ending a grand saloon tradition on the site. Edgar Crilly, son of the developer of Crilly Court, bought the land and turned it into a park.

THE DELUXE GARDENS AND PADDY BAULER

Old Town was not left saloon-less, however, even though Prohibition killed the legal saloons in 1920. Over three thousand speakeasies continued to operate citywide, and village taverns met the demand for secret, if illegal, drinking. On North Avenue and Sedgwick Streets, Forty-third Ward alderman Paddy Bauler ran a lively establishment from which he dispensed both liquid refreshment and "favors for friends."

The nature of the saloon and the saloonkeeper changed after Prohibition. Both became more political. Politics was a natural progression for saloonkeepers because of the nature of their business. As was previously noted, in neighborhoods where literacy was low, the saloon was a gathering place for exchanging information, a safe for valuables, a telephone for emergencies, a free lunch, a place to cash paychecks and a restroom. A savvy saloonkeeper turned politician could turn these resources into votes. So it was with one Mathias J. (Paddy) Bauler and his DeLuxe Gardens Saloon.

The DeLuxe was favored by Old Town residents from Prohibition until 1967. The saloon occupied the former premises of the Immigrant State Bank, which went under in the stock market crash of 1929. A.J. Liebling, in *Chicago: The Second City*, described it "as sedate a groggery as you will come upon in the City of Chicago." The DeLuxe kept all the former

Paddy Bauler's DeLuxe Gardens Saloon on the southeast corner of Sedgwick and North Avenue. *ICHI-21459. Photo by Sigmund J. Osly, 1967.*

bank's accoutrements: high ceilings, grilles barring the way to the vaults and imposing marble décor.

There was no entertainment—not even a dice girl—in the establishment. But patrons didn't go to the DeLuxe for entertainment—or even to enjoy a shot and a beer. They went to pass the time with "Paddy" Bauler, alderman of the Forty-third Ward.

MATHIAS J. (PADDY) BAULER): 1890–1977

There has probably never been a more colorful alderman or a more experienced saloonkeeper than Paddy (nobody called him Mathias) Bauler. He was to the tavern born. From the time he was old enough to pull a tap or pour a shot, he worked behind the bar in his father's saloon. During Prohibition, he ran a speakeasy at the corner of Willow and Howe Streets, where Old Town denizens rubbed shoulders with the rich and famous: Rudy Vallee (movie star and crooner), Anton Cermak (politician) and Edith Rockefeller McCormick (wealthy socialite). He graduated from this job to owning his own saloon at North Avenue and Sedgwick, where he held court from 9:00 a.m. to 11:00 p.m. with one or more of his "executive assistants." He was always available in case someone had a brother who had been arrested or a relative who needed to be admitted to the hospital without a lot of red tape. "You gotta keep in touch" was his motto.

Paddy's first political job was as a timekeeper in the Cook County treasurer's office. He was elected to the city council as alderman of the Forty-third Ward in 1933. He won every aldermanic race but one for the next thirty-four years. He used to boast, "Every election comes up and they put some egghead against me. When the election is over, yours truly comes back to the city council."

The enormously popular Paddy was not Irish, as many thought from his nickname. In fact, his roots had more in common with Old Town's original German community. His father was born in Germany and his mother in Illinois, of German parents. By the time Paddy became alderman in 1933, his ward was so ethnically mixed that there was no particular benefit in declaring himself to be Irish rather than German. Among politicians of his time, however, the rule was: when in doubt, be Irish.

Paddy was a huge man with a chubby pink face. When he first began courting the attention of Mayor Cermak, he used to roll about on the floor at city hall in wrestling matches with himself to make His Honor laugh. There are a lot of good stories circulating about Paddy. According to one, a few nights before Christmas 1933, he shot a policeman who wanted to be served a drink after hours. Paddy had locked up and was depositing the receipts from a Forty-third Ward Democratic benefit show in the old bank's vault. The policeman banged on the door and, using foul language, demanded to be admitted. Paddy went out to quiet him down. "Johnny, why have I got this coming to me for?" he asked. "I never done nothing to you." Then he drew his gun and shot the policeman (not fatally). The word in Old Town was that no one ever used bad language outside the DeLuxe or tried to get a drink after hours following that incident.

That's one version of the story. Here is the "hidden" version. It is entirely possible that the policeman did demand an after-hours drink from Paddy—but he also called the saloonkeeper a "big Dutch pig who ought to be back on a garbage wagon." That's when Paddy shot him. He was not only offended by the slur to him personally, but also many of his precinct captains were garbage collectors, and insulting their profession was unforgivable.

The Forty-third Ward was one of the most diverse in the city. On the east, it took in the Gold Coast, including the famed Ambassador hotels and the Cardinal's mansion. Its southern border was a slum, which later became Cabrini Green. At its center was the old Cabbage Patch community—renamed North Town after the Fire—containing a German-language movie house, a few German restaurants and numerous bars and businesses. The population was made up of Japanese, Finns, Hungarians, Italians, Irish, Syrians, Armenians, Swedes and Poles. The physical appearance of the ward was as varied as its population. Parts looked like typical inner-city areas; others were more like the suburbs.

There were forty thousand votes in Paddy's ward, monitored by seventy-six precinct captains, each holding a city, state or county job. The alderman admitted that he had some "very nice jobs to give out"—paying from $250 to $350 a month. All a fellow had to do was keep track of the votes in his precinct and get out the Democratic votes when it counted. Paddy demanded to know within one percentage point how the vote would turn out in any given precinct. Anyone who failed to keep track of the votes was ousted.

Like any successful politician, Paddy took care of his people. If there was a hole in a front sidewalk, a precinct captain would ring the doorbell about a week before an election and ask if the constituent was interested in having it fixed. There was never a doubt about what it would take to have the repair done.

Then, as now, getting voters out for local elections could be difficult, but Paddy had his methods. He would call in a precinct captain and ask how many voters he thought he could get to the polls. If the fellow answered with a low, but reasonable, figure, Paddy would hint that a better job and a little something extra for the kids might be found if the worker could manage at least 50 more votes. Usually, the individual managed to bring in at least 150 more. When Paddy was sure of a victory on election night, he would have a party for the entire ward. In his signature silk top hat and frock coat, he would twirl his cane and dance around the DeLuxe, singing, "Chicago, Chicago, that toddlin' town."

While the Gold Coast was part of the Forty-third Ward, it was not Paddy's favorite neighborhood. People there didn't need his extra favors and could not be relied on to do the organization work. Paddy observed that many Gold Coast residents were Republicans and were always complaining about dirty streets, bad lighting and not enough cops. "But when you come right down to it, " he said, "they only got one vote apiece, just like everybody else."

Bauler was a firm believer that one favor deserved another, and he had no patience for reformers. He called them "political science kids," and he let them know in no uncertain terms that "Chicago ain't ready for reform." He told everyone, "Them guys in the black suits and narrow ties, them Ivy League types, them goo-goos—they think the whole thing is on the square...People want service," he said," not reform." He saw his job in very simple terms: collect the garbage, repair the streets and clean the sidewalks and people will vote for you.

Journalists were aware of Paddy's activities. When Richard J. Daley was first elected mayor, narrowly defeating his reform opponent, it was noted by a few journalists that some Democratic precincts came through for him with nearly 100 percent of the vote. Bauler made the front page of one newspaper with a photograph of him dancing on a tabletop in the DeLuxe and a caption stating, "Chicago ain't ready for reform!"

Robert C. Nelson, a reporter for the *Christian Science Monitor*, published a series of exposés about Bauler in which he revealed many of his escapades. When the first story broke, Paddy phoned the reporter and exclaimed, "Robby Boy, Robby Boy, those were awful things you said about me. But I got to hand it to you. It's the truth." Later, Bauler invited Rob to his annual Christmas party, along with a number of other political journalists. During the course of the evening, he saw Paddy giving out envelopes to these reporters. When he got to Rob, he handed him an envelope that contained a sizable amount of cash. Rob gave it back. Bauler was astonished, indicating that this was a first.

Paddy retired from the city council in 1967—one of the last of the saloon-keeping politicians. He died in 1977, about "twenty years too late," according to journalist William Brasher. His cronies were all dead or dying, his flamboyant style was out of date and his Forty-third Ward had become the domain of "reformers." One wonders if his son, Harry, heeded his admonition: "Harry, if anything happens to me, I don't want you to call the priest or the undertaker. Just get your ass down to the bank and get them deposit boxes!" Even if he had, he would not have profited greatly. Paddy never accumulated a lot of money. He spent it as fast as he made it, often on luxury trips to Europe. He left only about $140,000 in cash (he never had a checking account).

John Hall: A Modern Beer Baron

The demise of the old Wells Street saloons and the DeLuxe Gardens did not spell the end of the Old Town beer barons. The tradition is alive and well—and living on Orleans in the person of John Hall, beer baron and brewmaster extraordinaire. Here is his story.

John Hall and his wife, Pat, live in a wonderful Old Town row house that is one-third of the old St. James Congregational Church. The front of the house is virtually "hidden" on Orleans Street. It is the back that the

The Hall garden and rear view of their converted condominium. *Photo by Norman Baugher.*

public sees. Like many Old Town homeowners, the Halls (mostly Pat, who is a horticulturalist) have turned this area into a nature preserve. The space is dominated by a huge spruce tree surrounded by colorful plantings that change with the seasons. In the spring, there are tulips, daffodils, pansies and hyacinth. Come summer, these are replaced with impatiens, fuchsias, hibiscus and geraniums. Fall brings a plethora of chrysanthemums. As was done by so many Old Towners in the past, the Halls make good use of their garden by entertaining friends and neighbors there in the summer.

Inside, the house is very traditional; its furnishings include a large century-old bookcase brought over from a French chateau, a vintage marble fireplace and granite pillars. Hanging on the living room wall is a painting of John's grandmother, surrounded by paintings of Old Town and a lovely old New England tapestry. The windows on the Orleans entrance overlook St. Michael's Church. The rear deck leads to their garden.

A Pair of Transplants

Both John and Pat came to Chicago from Iowa. John's brother and sister moved here first. John came to visit when he was a teenager and knew that he, too, wanted to live here. He and Pat met at the University of Iowa, where she was studying to be an English teacher. They married, and John came to Chicago looking for a job. He found one with the Container Corporation, which immediately sent him back to Iowa. But John kept angling for a transfer. It came two years later.

The Halls didn't come to Old Town but to suburban Hinsdale. Pat raised their children there, and John commuted to Chicago for more than twenty years. John's job with Container Corporation required extensive travel. On his many trips to Europe, he developed an interest in European beers, which he had shipped back to the States for his personal consumption. He became especially fond of specialty beers and started reading up on their production—moving closer and closer to becoming a brewer. In the late 1980s, when it became obvious that Container Corporation was going to be sold, John decided he was ready for a career change. A business trip to Texas confirmed his decision. He had boarded a plane for Chicago when a bad storm forced the plane to remain on the runway for hours. Frustrated and tired, John picked up a magazine and started to browse through. Call it fate, but the lead article was about craft beers and their creators. Then and there, he decided to open a brewery—and Goose Island was born.

When he returned to Chicago, he took the steps necessary to make his dream a reality. He started looking for a spot to build his brewery. He solicited ideas from other small brewers in the area. He put his MBA degree and Container Corporation experience to work and devised a sound business plan. After a year and a half, when everything was in place, Goose Island opened its doors.

After their children graduated from college, the Halls were finally ready to end the commuting and move to Chicago. Pat started house hunting in the city. Though her requirements were simple—a front and back door and a garden—it was nine years before she and John finally found what they wanted. One look at the rehabbed old church was all they needed. In 1997, they became Old Towners.

CARRYING ON A GRAND TRADITION

Old Town and John Hall were made for each other. John follows a long line of brewers who formed an important part of the community's history. In 1852, when Michael Diversey opened the Diversey and Lill Brewery, saloons could be found on almost every street in Old Town. They served as social clubs, gathering places and a lifeline to the old country for the workingmen in the community. In 1855, Klungel's Lager Beer Saloon was built at 1623 North Wells and became a favorite tavern for the German population. Frederick Wacker, a real estate mogul who built Old Town's most prestigious house on Lincoln Park West, was a brewer, as was Old Town resident Francis J. Dewes. Peter Hand, with partners John Heuer and Dr. Joseph Watry, opened the Peter Hand Brewing Company in Old Town. Their Meister Brau beer is still distributed. John Hall is a giant among this auspicious group of brewers. His son, Greg, now considered by many the most innovative person in American brewing, joined his father, first as a minimum-wage employee and then as CBO (chief beer officer) for the company.

Goose Island beers were an instant hit with both Old Town beer lovers and devotees throughout Chicago. Many serious beer drinkers had been looking for specialty beers produced by microbreweries and at brewpubs. Goose Island led the way for those microbreweries. It opened two brewpubs and, over time, hired 120 regular employees. Its specialty beers are now sold in wine and liquor stores, supermarkets and bars/restaurants nationwide. From a single entry in the handcrafted field, the Goose Island output has grown to a pantheon of favorites: Honkers Ale (so named by Pat), India Pale Ale, 312 Urban Wheat, Goose Island White City, Sofie (named for the Halls' granddaughter), Goose Island Oatmeal Stout, Goose Island Reserve, Goose Island Pepe Nero, Goose Island Pere Jacques, Goose Island Summertime and Bourbon County Coffee Stout. King Henry (named for the Halls' grandson) will make its appearance in 2011. Goose Island root beer is the soft drink of choice among all root beer lovers, young and old.

In the tradition of the old neighborhood pubs, Goose Island has two brewpubs in the city where a devoted group of regulars and visitors gather to socialize, dine and, of course, enjoy their favorite brew. For the past several years, Goose Island has held theme dinners to which patrons are invited. Each course of the outstanding meal is paired with an appropriate beer. Diners are always amazed at how perfectly beer accompanies food. John says it is much easier and more interesting to combine beer and food than wine and food. These dinners are eagerly anticipated and draw fans from all over the country. They are always sold out.

In 2011, Goose Island sold its brewery to Anheuser-Busch—not because business was bad but because it was too good. According to brewmaster Greg Hall, demand for their specialty beers had grown beyond their capacity to serve wholesale partners, retailers and beer lovers. Under the sales agreement Anheuser-Busch will be able to manufacture the beers in the quantity needed to meet the increased demand. The sale does not mean the end of Goose Island in Chicago or the end of John Hall's career as one of Chicago's most successful brewers—far from it. Goose Island will remain an independent company within the Anheuser-Bush enterprise, and John Hall will continue as CEO. Brewing of the Goose Island products will continue to be centered in Chicago, and sales and marketing will go through John. "Goose Island will become stronger and will be able to do more things, not just as a business, but as a part of Chicago," he maintains.

So farewell and hail. And let the good times roll on.

4

A Hot Time in Old Town

The Great Chicago Fire of 1871

*If one could make alive again for other people some cobwebbed skein of old
dead intrigues and breathe breath and character into dead names and stiff
portraits. That is history to me.*
—George Macaulay Trevelyan

Tragedy struck Chicago and the Cabbage Patch in 1871 with the outbreak
of the Great Fire, arguably the greatest disaster of its kind in American
history. Given the construction materials of streets and buildings at the time,
one could almost have predicted the fire. The city had fifty-five miles of
planked streets. Wooden bridges formed the passages across rivers and canals.
Roofs were made of tar and pine chips, both highly flammable, and large
quantities of hay and straw were kept throughout the city as feed for horses.

Though Chicago had an excellent fire department—185 men strong—the
steam-powered water pumpers were only a little more effective than the old
bucket brigades. Then, as now, the key to fighting fires effectively was rapid
response to alarms. To ensure that calls were answered quickly, watchmen
were on duty twenty-four/seven in a high cupola over the courthouse. Each
of the local departments throughout the city also had an observation tower.
When watchmen spotted flames, they notified firehouses of their location.

Had this system been working effectively when the Great Fire broke out, it
might have been contained in a small area, even though the wooden streets
and buildings covering the city were dried out by a blistering summer in
which little rain had fallen. But the system wasn't working.

Early Chicago fire engine, 1871. Model of the Frederick Gund from Company 14 used in the Great Chicago Fire. *ICHI 02665.*

On Saturday, October 7, 1871, a terrible fire started in a planing mill on Canal Street between Jackson and Van Buren Streets. It took nearly one hundred firefighters fifteen hours to extinguish the blaze, which spread over four city blocks. Several of the engines and hose carts were so badly damaged by that fire that they could not be used again without extensive repairs. To make matters worse, after all those hours of nonstop exertion, more than half of the 185-man firefighting force was unfit for duty. And the worst was yet to come.

Did She or Didn't She?

One cold night while we were all in bed,
Old Mother Leary left the lantern in the shed.
And when the cow kicked it over, she kicked her heels and said,
There'll be a hot time in the Old Town tonight.

A Hot Time in Old Town

Legend has it that the Great Chicago Fire started on the evening of October 8, 1871, when Mrs. O'Leary's cow kicked over the kerosene lantern in her barn while she was milking it. Maybe—and maybe not. Contemporary accounts agree that the fire did start in one of the outbuildings on Mrs. O'Leary's property at 137 DeKoven Street. No one is quite sure about the role played by the cow. Logically, it seems unusual that a woman who milked her cow every night would leave a lantern in a position where the animal could kick it. Most versions of the story also say that the lantern was behind the cow when it was kicked over. That is strange because cows do not kick backward. A clue to the mystery of the fire may lie in Mrs. O'Leary's statement that she heard an explosion when the lantern fell over—by whatever means—and that it ignited the hay. A burning kerosene lamp does not explode. But at the time of the fire, many Chicago companies selling kerosene had been accused of adding gasoline to it. If the kerosene in Mrs. O'Leary's lamp was mixed with gasoline, she might well have heard an explosion. Had there been gasoline in the mixture, the fire would have spread rapidly and, unchecked, would have burned out of control.

Other possible explanations about the cause of the fire, excluding the cantankerous cow, might be that lightning struck the barn or that a disgruntled, drunken neighbor took vengeance on the O'Learys for whatever reason. Or perhaps raucous tenants accidentally dropped a lantern or something flammable. However it happened, the fire broke out early in the evening of October 8 and burned for twenty minutes before the first watchman turned in an alarm. That alarm failed to register. By the time another watchman in a distant fire tower saw the flames and dispatched the company to DeKoven Street, the fire had been raging for thirty minutes and had spread to adjacent buildings.

More companies responded, but seven were sent to wrong locations. When they finally arrived at the correct address, the fire was virtually unstoppable. By 2:30 a.m., fed by southwest winds, the inferno had jumped the Chicago River and was roaring northward.

With the exception of the Water Tower and pumping station at Chicago Avenue and Pine Street (now Michigan Avenue), most of the North District, including the Cabbage Patch, consisted of small wooden shops and cottages—fodder for the fire. The Water Tower survived the flames. The pumping station did not—so the city lost its water supply. The fire was capricious in its destruction. The Chicago Historical Society at Dearborn and Ontario Streets, said to be the most fireproof building in Chicago, burned to the ground. But the Mahlon Ogden mansion (he was the brother of Mayor William B. Ogden) on Walton and Dearborn Streets (now the site of the Newberry Library) was saved. Ogden's neighbor, Ezra B. McCogg, watched his house go up in flames, but not one window in the greenhouse was broken.

As the fire spread through the north side, one Chicagoan observed, "You couldn't see anything but fire—no sky, no clouds, no stars, nothing but fire. It was like a tornado of fire." Of course, mayhem ensued. Looters plundered goods from deserted shops. Bridges collapsed under the weight of hundreds of persons running for their lives. One woman knelt in the street with a crucifix in front of her face looking for divine deliverance. She was struck and killed by a runaway carriage. Household possessions loaded onto carts by desperate owners were burning even as drivers raced to safety. Masses huddled in the shallow water along the shore of Lake Michigan. Others sought shelter in empty grave sites of the old City Cemetery at the south end of what is now Lincoln Park. Flames created temperatures so high that plate glass windows cracked, iron and steel melted and limestone construction blocks disintegrated.

Fleeing the burning city along the lakefront and through the old Chicago City Cemetery, located just south of North Avenue. *ICHI 02881-9. Engraving sketch by Theodore Davis.*

A Hot Time in Old Town

As the fire approached St. Michael's Church, the bells began to toll. Parishioners removed the large wooden crucifix from the altar, as well as Bibles, candelabra and statues. They buried them in the church grounds as quickly as they could. Nuns and priests loaded the hand-carved Stations of the Cross, vestments and altar cloths onto a wagon and sent them to Rosehill, outside the city limits.

The fire was not brought under control until the evening of October 9, 1871. Since there were so few buildings north of Fullerton, the city's northern boundary, there was nothing left to burn. A heavy rain began to fall during the night, and by Tuesday morning, October 10, the fire was out, except for some coal piles and rubble heaps that smoldered for months.

In three days, the fire had devastated an area of more than three square miles—from Taylor Street north to Fullerton and west to the Chicago River. At its height, flames were seen as far away as Des Plaines, twenty miles from Chicago. More than one-third of the city was destroyed, including 17,450 structures, mostly on the north side. The entire downtown area—department stores, wholesale warehouses, the board of trade building and hotels—burned to the ground in one night. Over $1 million in currency, presumably protected by three inches of boilerplate and a wall of brick in the post office and customhouse, was incinerated in the fire's three-thousand-degree heat. The same was true of currency in the city's banks. At least three hundred people died, and ninety thousand were left homeless. Ironically, Mrs. O'Leary's cottage, south of the cow barn, was undamaged.

For weeks, relief carts carrying bread and meat moved through the Cabbage Patch and up Armitage as far as Central Street. Within the community, only the Hanselman family managed to save anything. The chairs and doors, which they had buried in a hole in the backyard, were found intact and were used to furnish their new home at 1814 North Orleans. Mr. Hanselman's favorite black walnut armchair took its accustomed place in the front room. The only north side residence left standing, other than Ogden's mansion, was a frame cottage in the 2100 block of Hudson Avenue belonging to a newly married policeman named Richard Bellinger, the site of a hidden story.

THE CIDER HOUSE RUSE

Richard Bellinger had recently built the small white house for his wife and was desperate to save it. He raked up all the dry leaves in his yard and ripped

Home of Richard Bellinger, 2121 North Hudson, the only house in Old Town to survive the Great Chicago Fire. *Photo by Carolyn Blackmon.*

up the wooden sidewalk, picket fence and front steps. He covered his roof with blankets and rugs and propped a ladder against the side of the house. Now, as we know, the legend of Mrs. O'Leary's cow having started the Great Fire of 1871 just will not go away. True or not, it is a great story. But there is another story—almost as good—about the fire and Policeman Richard Bellinger's house. Here is how that one goes.

Saving the little cottage at 2121 North Hudson is a story of love, a man's devotion to his wife and his attachment to the home he built for her. It is also the story of how one man defied nature and won. According to that story, started locally and repeated for years all over the country, Bellinger saved his house by pouring on generous dousings of cider. Although he was fortunate enough to have had a small quantity of water on hand when the fire approached his house, that supply was soon gone. He tore up the wooden sidewalk and used water from the ground beneath to keep the flames away. But even that wasn't enough. As the flames came closer and sparks fell on the roof, Bellinger was desperate. He had to have more water—even a bucketful. And then he remembered that he had a barrel of cider in the cellar that he had put by to drink in the coming winter. Deciding that the red devil threatening to devour his house needed the cider worse than he did, Bellinger went down to get the cider barrel and started pouring it on the endangered spots cup by cup until his house was safe. For years afterward, his house was known as the cider house.

Then, one day in 1915, a little white-haired old lady walked up the front steps and knocked on the door at 2131 North Hudson. By then, the owner was one Joseph Kirschten. Mrs. Kirschten, wife of the owner, opened the door. The old lady identified herself as the widow of Policeman Bellinger and asked if she might look inside the place that was once her home. "I was glad to show her the house," Mrs. Kirschten said later. "She looked around eagerly, felt the old sliding doors, went into the basement and touched the window frames. She appeared to be happy. The visit seemed to bring back memories of her girlhood romance. And then she told the true story of how her cottage was saved."

On the night of the fire, Richard Bellinger—some say he was a captain of police—was determined to save his house. He thought his chances were good because his was the only house on the block. When the flames approached, he put blankets on the roof and climbed up and down the ladder pouring on bucketsful of water from his cistern to wet down the blankets. When the cistern was empty, he got more water from a dugout that belonged to a small truck farmer across the street. Then he brought water from what was at the time called the Ten-Mile Ditch, a block or two east of his house, parallel to North Clark Street. He and his brother-in-law set up a bucket brigade, bringing water from all of these available sources. They battled the flames all night long, and by morning, the danger had passed.

Good neighbors that they were, Bellinger and his wife furnished food and shelter to twenty-one persons who had been made homeless by the fire until they were able to get outside relief. "The story that my husband put out the fire with cider was not true," said Mrs. Bellinger. "We did have a barrel of cider in the basement, sure enough, but we didn't use it because we were able to get enough water from across the street."

Today, there is a plaque on the front façade of the house that commemorates the house's survival. But that's not the only relic of the fire. There is also a framed religious picture hanging on the upstairs wall that had been saved when Kirschten's mother fled from their home near North Avenue and Wells Street. Mr. Kirschten was only three years old at the time.

A CABBAGE PATCH RESIDENT SURVIVES THE FIRE

Most families living in the North Division went to bed on the night of October 8, 1871, with no idea that a fire was burning out of control in the West Division. Included in this group were the Germans, Irish, Bohemians and Scandinavians of what was then the Sixteenth Ward, which included Old Town. Patrick Webb's was one of those families.

Patrick Webb was a day laborer for the Northwestern Railroad who lived on Church Street. He was awakened by the clamor of fire bells about 2:00 a.m. on October 9. He groaned, knowing he had to go to work in another three hours. Deciding that his family was in no danger, since the fire that had broken out on October 7 and destroyed sixteen acres to the south and west of his neighborhood had missed his neighborhood completely, he turned over and went back to sleep. He got up at 5:00 a.m. and went off to work. As late as 9:00 a.m., the fire had only spread as far as Oak and LaSalle Streets, so he was confident that any danger to his house was remote at best. He was wrong.

At 10:00 a.m., Patrick got word at his job that the wind had changed and was driving the flames directly north. His foreman told him to go home. By that time, the fire was raging up Wells Street. Patrick stopped on his way home to help evacuate some of his relatives to safety. When he got to his own house, he was relieved to find it intact, and he believed it would be spared. He was wrong again. By then, the Chicago Avenue Bridge was in flames, along with a nearby distillery. The fire was on a course leading directly to his home.

It was much too late for the Webbs to hire any kind of cart or carriage to take them and their possessions to safety—they probably couldn't have afforded one anyway given the exorbitant rates being charged. The family began frantically digging pits and burying as much of their household goods and clothing as possible. They had only gone down three feet when they hit water. Deciding that water was better than flames, they threw in whatever they could. Their efforts were cut short by sparks and flying debris. They literally had to run for their lives.

But they had no place to go. To make matters worse, having buried their clothes, the family was not prepared to spend a night outside. They had no other option, however. Patrick, his wife and their four children passed the night of October 9 huddled with hundreds of other unfortunate families on the open prairie. During the night, it began to rain, increasing their misery.

On Tuesday, October 10, the rain finally put out the fire. About 5:00 a.m., a Lutheran church that had been spared opened its doors to the crowd, and

Patrick's family took shelter inside. They were given food and blankets, but Patrick took little comfort from the assistance. "I felt real bad," he said. "I considered myself a beggar." When he went back to the site where his home had been, he found the house still smoldering. The possessions he had buried in their watery grave had also been burned beyond saving. At fifty-eight, after what he described as a life of "hard work and sobriety," Patrick Webb was nearly destitute.

Luckily, he had taken out insurance from a company that was supposed to protect homeowners. The company finally settled his claim for about $30. His real help came from the Chicago Relief and Aid Society, which gave the family $90 worth of lumber, plus $100 cash, along with coal, provisions and clothing. With this help, the Webbs rebuilt and became part of the new Cabbage Patch, soon to be renamed North Town.

There are many other stories documenting the grit and determination with which Chicagoans in general and Old Towners in particular set about rebuilding their city. While wealthier citizens could recoup more readily than the day laborers of the Sixteenth Ward, all pitched in and refused to let their city and their neighborhood die.

5

From Resting Place to Recreation Space

The historian has before him a jigsaw puzzle from which many pieces have disappeared. These gaps can be filled only by his imagination.
—*Gaetano Salvemini*

Today, one of the most beautiful sites in Old Town is Lincoln Park, located on the banks of Lake Michigan from Ardmore Avenue in Edgewater south to the Ohio Street Beach. The area is well known for the Lincoln Park Zoo, a free zoo that is open year round and home to more than twelve hundred animals, including polar bears, penguins, gorillas, reptiles and big cats. Two sections of the zoo have been set-aside for children: the Children's Zoo and the Farm-in-the-Zoo, a working reproduction of a midwestern farm. At this farm, children can feed and interact with animals. They can also view live demonstrations of farm work, such as milking the cows. In 2010, the zoo created a wildlife marsh habitat with a nature boardwalk. Other important features of Lincoln Park are the famous conservatory, offering year-round displays of plants from around the world; the Alfred Caldwell Lily Pool, a historic example of Prairie School landscape architecture; and the Peggy Notebaert Nature Museum, featuring a live butterfly house and a green home demonstration. At the south end of the park is the internationally acclaimed Chicago History Museum, dedicated to everything about Chicago's human history.

This magnificent site did not begin life as a park but as a cemetery—the Chicago City Cemetery. Established in 1843, this early Chicago graveyard stretched from Armitage Avenue to Kinzie Street, then the southern edge of Chicago's city limits. The City Cemetery was subdivided into three sections: a potters' field, a Catholic cemetery and a cemetery for the general population. A Jewish Burial Society bought almost an acre of the land in 1846 for burial of its people. Four years later, the city added twelve more acres by purchasing the adjacent estate of Jacob Milleman, who had died of cholera. Milleman's heirs later contested this sale and won a $75,000 suit against the city.

Before the establishment of this cemetery, Chicago settlers made some poor decisions about the burial of their loved ones. Some put their kin in backyards; others selected sites too close to the banks of the Chicago River. When the downtown area was dug up to lay foundations for skyscrapers after the Great Fire, developers were nonplussed to come upon bones of some early inhabitants. In other instances, Chicagoans were shocked to see remains of their loved ones floating down the Chicago River after a heavy rain.

Not too many years after the cemetery was opened, north side residents began complaining about conditions on the grounds. A huge population growth in the city resulted in overcrowding and a series of cholera epidemics. People feared that outbreaks of disease and contamination of water would become frequent occurrences. In addition, they were angry that the city morgue and a holding place for epidemic victims—a pest house—were also located on the grounds. Cabbage Patch residents appealed to their alderman, Lawrence Proudfoot, to have the cemetery closed and remains moved to another site. Proudfoot began a twenty-year protest to change the site from resting place to recreation space. He was joined in this effort by public health reformers who were conducting a campaign against unsanitary burial practices. In 1864, the cemetery was closed. The city council passed an ordinance forbidding the sale of any other cemetery plots within the city limits. At the same time, aldermen approved a plan to relocate the existing graves to the "suburban" areas of Graceland, Rosehill and Oak Woods. Though outside the city limits, the relocated cemeteries were easily accessible to residents via Chicago's improved transportation system: a steam railroad commuter service, a horse-drawn street railway system and a span bridge over the Chicago River at Rush Street (publicized as the first iron bridge west of the Alleghenies). The original cemetery site was decreed a park and was named after the assassinated president Abraham Lincoln.

Following the official closing of the City Cemetery, the graves were dug up and coffins were moved north. Roman Catholic families chose to send their dead to Calvary Cemetery in Evanston or St. Boniface in Chicago. Jewish families sent their loved ones to a site at Belmont and Clark Streets. As was mentioned earlier, some of the empty sites had been left open before the development of the park—and provided shelter to many of the terrified citizens fleeing north from the south side during the Great Fire of 1871.

Today, Old Town residents and visitors can still visit two monuments from the old cemetery. Both are shrouded in mystery. One is that of Ira Couch and his family, who are buried in an imposing mausoleum at the southern end of the park near the Chicago History Museum. Couch was the owner of one of the city's leading hotels: the Tremont House. There are conflicting theories as to why this tomb remains when other markers and burial containers were removed. The most popular explanation, put forth in 1937, is that the tomb is so big and so heavy that it would have cost over $3,000 to have it moved. Plus, its great stones are fastened together with copper rivets, so there was no way of dismantling and moving it without blowing it up or wrecking it completely. Park commissioners determined to let it remain and planted trees around it. There is also speculation that commissioners were under pressure from the influential members of the Couch family to let it

Couch Mausoleum, one of two known surviving grave sites in Lincoln Park from the old Chicago City Cemetery. *Photo by Carolyn Blackmon.*

stay. Some years later, the Supreme Court of the United States ruled that the burial lot belonged to the dead, not the living, effectively ending the controversy and the objections of successive park commissioners.

The second remaining monument is that of David Kennison, who claimed to be a 116-year-old survivor of the Boston Tea Party—and therein lies a story.

David Kennison—Was He or Wasn't He?

The story of David Kennison is a fascinating one. Kennison arrived in Chicago in 1840, claiming to be a veteran of the War of 1812. That was not his only claim. He also swore that he was the last survivor of the Boston Tea Party and a soldier in the Revolutionary War. He attracted such attention that when he died in 1852, Chicago gave him one of the grandest funerals the city had ever witnessed and placed his remains in the old City Cemetery. In an article entitled "David Kennison and the Chicago Sting," Albert Overton wrote, "Muffled drums beat a slow marching pace for the magnificent parade—a funeral cortege to honor what was thought to be a well-known Revolutionary War hero. Actually, they were escorting the mortal remains of one of the most colorful imposters ever to take the city of Chicago." Another Kennison chronicler speculated, "It is likely Chicagoans were so desperate for a link to the Revolution and so credulous that they embraced Kennison who migrated to the burgeoning city advertising himself as 112 years old, a participant at the Boston Tea Party, and a veteran of every battle from Lexington to Yorktown. In reality, Kennison was only nine or so in 1773, which put him in his 80s when he died." The "facts" of his story bear some examination.

First, there is the matter of his birthday. At one point, he claimed to be 59 years old in 1835—which would have him born in 1776. In 1840, he gave his age as 82—indicating that he was born in 1758. When he came to Chicago from Maine, he stated that he was born in 1736, making him 104 years old. So when was he really born? All that is known for certain is that his name pops on and off the U.S. pension rolls through the mid-1800s.

His accounts of his war experiences are also questionable. In 1848, he told a Chicago newspaper reporter that he had been present when Cornwallis surrendered at Yorktown in 1781. A few years later, he swore to a magazine writer that his company had been in a skirmish at Saratoga Springs. In that encounter, he said, he and his fellow soldiers were captured by about three hundred Mohawk Indians. According to his story, the Mohawks held him prisoner for more than a year and a half—about the end of which time peace was declared, making it impossible for him to have been at Yorktown. He also said that he fought under a General Montgomery, who died leading an American invasion in Canada in 1775. There is no record of Kennison having been involved in that campaign.

There's more. The imaginative Mr. Kennison wrote that during the Battle of Bunker Hill, "I helped roll barrels filled with sand and stone down the hill as the British came up." It was later learned that the so-called sand and stone barrels were used as part of the fortification of Dorchester Heights, which occurred some months later, and they were never rolled.

It is true that Kennison's name was among those of a list of soldiers stationed at Fort Dearborn in the early 1800s. There is no evidence, however, that he fought at Fort Dearborn or that he was there when the fort fell in 1812. Since Fort Dearborn later became the City of Chicago, there is some speculation that Kennison returned to the area in 1848, hoping to find some fame and support in his old age.

Nonetheless, in 1903, a group of Revolutionary War buffs and a number of Kennison admirers decided to erect a monument, a huge boulder, marking the approximate spot where they thought he was buried. They installed a commemorative bronze plaque that read, "In memory of David Kennison, the last survivor of the Boston Tea Party, who died in Chicago February 24, 1852, aged 115 years, 3 mos., 17 days, and is buried near this spot." In 1972, vandals stole the plaque and spray painted the boulder with graffiti. The monument stood bare for two and a half years. The original bronze plaque was replaced with an aluminum replica in 1974.

In 1921, the David Kennison chapter of the Daughters of the American Revolution was formed. It held gatherings at the boulder every year on Memorial Day, Flag Day, George Washington's Birthday and the anniversary of the Boston Tea Party.

Though David Kennison did indeed live a long and colorful life, it is unlikely that he was as old as he claimed to be. Historians have determined that he was approximately 85 years old when he died. Chicagoans claim he was 115. Using National Archives documents, including pension files, census records dating back to 1790 and Bounty Land files, the aforementioned Albert Overton debunked many of Kennison's claims with simple logic. "Actually," he wrote, "he was about seven years old at the time of the Tea

The boulder marking the entrance of the potters' field section of the old City Cemetery. Kennison claimed to be the last survivor of the Boston Tea Party, a claim later disproved. *Photo by Carolyn Blackmon.*

Party, saw no Revolutionary War service, and was about 85 years old, not 115 when he died."

Whatever you choose to believe, stop by and visit the Kennison Boulder when you're in the neighborhood. And let your imagination take it from there.

A LITTLE CURRENT HISTORY—NOT SO HIDDEN

Another aspect of Lincoln Park's history has to do with the appearance of gangs on the north side in the 1960s. The Young Lords of Lincoln Park held neighborhood sit-ins and takeovers of area institutions. They were protesting the displacement of Latinos by Mayor Richard J. Daley's urban renewal policies. The park was also the scene of a series of violent protests that took place during the 1968 Democratic National Convention. These events took place in a number of park areas, including Grant Park, Old Town and Lincoln Park. Of the demonstrations, Abbie Hoffman, one of the leaders of the protests and a member of the famed Chicago 7, wrote:

I pointed out that it was in the best interests of the City to have us in Lincoln Park ten miles away from the Convention Hall. I said we had no intention of marching on the Convention Hall, that I didn't particularly think that politics in America could be changed by marches and rallies, that what we were presenting was an alternative life style, and we hoped that people of Chicago would come up and mingle in Lincoln Park and see what we were about.

One wonders what the ghosts of Ira Couch and David Kennison thought of the event.

6

HOLLYWOOD BY THE LAKE

We are never completely contemporaneous with our present. History advances in disguise; it appears onstage wearing a mask of the preceding scene, and we tend to lose the meaning of the play.
—*Regis Debray*

Hooray for Hollywood,
That screwy, ballyhooey Hollywood
Where any office boy or young mechanic can be a panic
With just a good looking pan
And any bar maid can be a star main
If she dances with or without a fan.
—*Johnny Mercer/Richard Whiting, 1937*

In the early 1900s, Chicago became, for a very brief period, the motion picture capital of the world, and Old Town was an important part of that fame. Not only did the city become a thriving center for motion picture production, but also a new viewing venue was born: the nickelodeon theater. By 1907, Chicago had 116 nickelodeons, which projected film directly onto a screen instead of into a box. Charging five cents for admission, hence the name nickelodeon, these theaters operated out of storefronts, club basements and other handy locations. A piano player provided musical background to what was taking place on the screen.

The public flocked to the new entertainment centers. Not only did nickelodeons revolutionize the filmmaking industry by becoming the place to go for entertainment, but they also provided a boon to the economy by creating a number of motion picture–related jobs. Chicago businesses that wanted capitalize on the growing popularity of movies started advertising in the *Daily News*, the *Tribune* and other widely read periodicals. Aspiring musicians found opportunities for work. A gentleman by the name of Charles Quinn set up shop at 59 East Van Buren Street and offered his services as an arranger for motion picture music, and several pianists advertised their willingness to perform in "first class movie theaters." Drama teachers advertised for would-be movie stars by promising motion picture instruction. Actors were attracted by the promise of instruction by a competent director who had been connected with feature productions. Business was good.

GEORGE SPOOR, "BRONCO" BILLY ANDERSON AND THE ESSANAY FILM MANUFACTURING COMPANY

You oughta' be in pictures
You're wonderful to see
You oughta' be in pictures
Oh what a hit you would be.
—Edward Heyman/Dana Suesse

George Spoor did not begin his career as a movie producer. In 1895, he owned and operated a newspaper stand—not a very high-paying job—in the old Chicago and Northwestern Station, then located at Kinzie Avenue and Wells Streets. To make ends meet, he worked the box office—also not a very lucrative position—at the Waukegan Opera House in downtown Waukegan, Illinois. Fate intervened in the form of one Edwin Hill Amet, an employee of the Waukegan Scale Works. Amet was working on a device to project motion pictures onto a screen instead of into a box. He had already made a modest reputation for himself by inventing a penny scale that printed out a card giving a person's weight. But his ambitions were greater than penny scales. He wanted to make a splash in the movie world with his projection machine.

Hill figured Spoor would have inside information on what was going on in the entertainment world, so he approached him with his plan. Spoor was interested and didn't let on that his knowledge of the industry was pretty much confined to the ticket booth. What he saw impressed him. The problem was that he had no money to invest in its manufacture. He asked Amet how much he thought it would take to complete the projector and was told it would be about sixty-five dollars. Spoor gave Amet all his ready cash: twenty-five dollars.

Amet completed his projector, which he called a "Magniscope," the following year. He did not go on to make his fortune with it, however. Thinking that the movie fad would run its course, he sold his invention to Spoor. Spoor's vision was more in keeping with the times. He established his own company, the National Film Renting Company, at 62 North Clark Street and started distributing films and projectors nationwide. Soon, he was able to close the newspaper stand and live off the profits of his new venture. Within ten years, he had turned his twenty-five-dollar investment into a modest fortune.

Spoor's early films were small documentaries of American life. He photographed streetcars rushing down crowded city streets, athletic events, cops and robbers chase scenes and even people walking. He was able to hire staff to assist with production and distribution, two of whom later became well known in their own right: Donald J. Bell and Albert Howell (Bell and Howell).

Another would-be film entrepreneur—G.M. "Bronco" Billy Anderson, a well-known cowboy actor and stunt man—paid a visit to Spoor and offered his services. The two created a partnership. Spoor would take over distribution of the films, and Anderson would be in charge of production. They named their new venture the Peerless Film Manufacturing Company (this name was later changed to the Essanay Film Manufacturing Company, after the initials of the two partners, *S* and *A*). They moved their headquarters to 501 North Wells Street.

The company's first film was called *An Awful Skate* and was shot on the sidewalk in front of the studio. Anderson directed the movie. Its star was a cross-eyed comedian called Ben Turpin, a fascinating character with permanently crossed eyes and a walrus mustache. Following the company's documentary format, Turpin skated up and down Wells Street in a top hat and tails, bumping into bystanders. People who ran after him usually ended up in the feature as extras. For his "acting" efforts, the comedian earned fifteen dollars a week. The salary also included his working as a janitor for the company. Turpin's antics were so popular that he became a star of silent films and worked with all the leading comic actors of the time: including

Charlie Chaplin and Laurel and Hardy. Lloyds of London even insured his eyes for $1 million in the event they ever became uncrossed. Almost as popular as Turpin were the Keystone Kops, a zany group of policemen who spent their reel time chasing bad guys down Eugenie Street and up Crilly Court in Old Town.

Essanay's movies became the rage of the moviegoing public. As audiences grew more sophisticated and wanted realistic backgrounds, Anderson and Spoor took the company on location—to Rogers Park, where they shot *The Life of Jesse James*, and to Starved Rock, where they filmed outdoor documentaries. They expanded their quarters and built a huge studio at 1345 West Argyle that housed three shooting stages, a carpentry shop, storage areas for props and wardrobe, a processing room, a publicity department and stars' dressing rooms. The company had a very sophisticated lighting system that employed both artificial and natural lights. One of its lighting technicians later went to Hollywood and became a successful director, as well as an inventor of the mercury-vapor light system.

Essanay coined the term "photoplay" to describe its motion pictures. And it hired an impressive group of actors that included the incredibly handsome Francis X. Bushman (for whom the famous Lincoln Park gorilla was later named—no resemblance), Wallace Beery, Gloria Swanson and the great Charlie Chaplin. With the exception of Chaplin, who had a penthouse suite at 2800 North Pinegrove (now Michigan Avenue), all the actors were housed in Old Town at the Crilly Court apartments. Bushman attracted the most attention. Starring in such hits as *His Friend's Wife*, *The Mail-Order Bride*, *White Roses*, *The House of Pride* and *When Soul Meets Soul*, he was every woman's dream. One State Street department store had to ask him not to shop there anymore because it couldn't accommodate the hordes of people who followed him through the door. Bushman met a young Chicago high school student while filming in Hyde Park. Her name was Beverly Bayne. The two became an item and were paired in a number of movies together. Eventually, they left Chicago for Hollywood and became contract players for Metro Studios. They were secretly married but did not let the public know for fear of damaging their careers.

Wallace Beery was another of Essanay's big stars. He had started his career as an elephant trainer for Ringling Brothers Circus. He went on to perform on Broadway and in vaudeville. When he signed with Essanay, he reverted to his circus days and paraded around as a drag queen in a dress and a blond wig as a Swedish maid named Sweedie. In the popular Sweedie series were such

The stars' address, Crilly Court, center of the Chicago movie-making industry in 1914.
Photo by Carolyn Blackmon.

audience pleasers as "Sweedie the Squatter," "Sweedie and her Dog" and "Sweedie Goes to College." Beery later met and married Gloria Swanson through Essanay. They went on to Hollywood, where both became famous.

Swanson's aunt was a friend of Spoor's, and in 1914, she took a tour of the Essanay studios. In true movie fashion, she was "discovered" there. A casting director saw her and paid her $3.25 to play the part of a wedding guest. That part led to another, and another and another. The studio eventually placed her on its "extras" list and guaranteed her $13.25 a week whether she worked or not—time and a half on Saturdays.

As big as Swanson and Beery were, they could not approach the fame of Charlie Chaplin. Chaplin's experience with Essanay was initially profitable for the company but frustrating to the actor. He was first signed by Anderson in California without Spoor's knowledge. Anderson promised the already-famous comedian $1,250 a week plus a $10,000 signing bonus. Chaplin agreed and got on a train for Chicago. Spoor, who had never even heard of Chaplin, was furious when he found out. At the time, the top comics were

Charlie Chaplin gets off the train in Chicago to star in his first feature comedy, *His New Job*, for Essanay Films. *CHS, DN 073431.*

only making $75 a week. Though he agreed to the contract, he made it a point to be out of town when Chaplin arrived. The front office had to pay the salary, but Chaplin had a terrible time getting his signing bonus.

Chaplin eventually settled into his penthouse suite and prepared to go to work. He went shopping on State Street and bought his signature baggy pants, oversized shoes and derby hat. The "Little Tramp" was about to make his Chicago debut. The film was called *His New Job* and revolved around a trouble-making handyman (Chaplin) and cross-eyed Ben Turpin. The plot had Chaplin creating havoc behind the scenes at a film studio, aided and abetted by Turpin. The two actors had great onstage and offstage chemistry and ended up making several other films together. Swanson was also in the film but did not get along with Chaplin. She hated his slapstick brand of comedy and hated being cast in the show, especially since she wanted to be a dramatic actress.

Spoor turned out dozens of twenty-minute shorts for about $1,000 apiece. Each film grossed more than $20,000. He stored his films in an icebox. During Essanay's heyday, Spoor threw lavish parties for his stars in the Crilly apartments and kept the street lively day and night. Though Chaplin attended the parties, he was not popular with his fellow actors, who resented his $1,250-a-week salary. Most of them only made about $15 per week—$20 if they worked on Saturdays.

After *His New Job* was completed, Chaplin refused to work with Spoor again. He left Chicago and went to work at Essanay's Hollywood studio until 1916, when his contract was up. Then he signed with another studio. Chaplin's defection, along with other legal problems, was the beginning of the end for Essanay. By 1918, the movie industry had moved to Hollywood, and Essanay closed. With the exception of Spoor, most of those connected with motion picture production went west. Spoor did not join the migration. He invested much of his personal fortune in a film process called "natural vision." But the coming of sound in motion pictures and the lack of investment capital brought about by the Great Depression doomed the process.

Down but not out, Spoor invested his remaining money in Texas oil fields and became a rich man again. He stayed in Chicago until his death in 1953 at the age of eighty-one. Anderson did not fare so well. He tried his hand at producing Broadway shows but was not successful. Then he went back to Hollywood and tried to revive his cowboy career, but copyright laws prevented him from using his "Bronco Billy" screen name. He left acting to become a director and made a few short comedies with Laurel and Hardy. But this stint did not last, and the once-famous "Bronco Billy" was reduced to doing a number of menial film jobs. He was virtually forgotten until 1957, when the Academy of Motion Picture Arts and Sciences awarded him an honorary Oscar for his contributions to the development of motion pictures.

As for Old Town and the movies, Chaplin's desertion didn't spell doom for the neighborhood as a popular filming location. In 1990, Goldie Hawn rented a house on Menomonee Street while filming a portion of *Bird on a Wire* in Chicago. Her daughter, the now-famous and glamorous Kate Hudson, annoyed diners in Canella's Restaurant on Wells Street by prancing around tables in a tutu. In 2000, Bonnie Hunt walked Minnie Driver and David Duchovny through the Old Town Art Fair and situated much of the action for *Return to Me* in Old Town's renowned Twin Anchors tavern. Mel Gibson (in a less controversial time of his career) walked on Crilly Court looking for the house of a wacky psychologist in *What Women Want*. Shelly Hack and Tom Mason virtually moved into the house at 1710 North Crilly Court to film the short-lived television series *Jack and Mike* in 1986. In addition to snarling Old Town traffic for weeks, they delighted neighborhood children with day-for-night shooting and fake rain scenes. Tom Cruise and Paul Newman took over the now-vanished Steak Joynt at 1610 North Wells (said to be one of the city's most haunted locations; more about that later) for their 1986 movie *The Color of Money*. Laurence Fishburne brought Vanessa Williams to Crilly Court (quite a popular little movie street, our Crilly Court) in 1997 to shoot *Hoodlum*. And, moving away from Crilly to Lincoln Park West in 2005, the popular television series *Prison Break* located a number of scenes in front of the famous Sullivan row houses (hunky star Wentworth Miller had more than a few young ladies' hearts fluttering). No doubt, there will be more.

7
GAY OLD TOWN

History, that little sewer where man loves to wallow.
—Francis Ponge

BOYS TOWN IN OLD TOWN

Crilly Court is not a street one would associate with illicit meetings, intrigue and subversive acts. Yet it was the scene of all of these for a very brief period in 1924. That was the year Henry Gerber rented a room in the old Queen Anne row house at 1710 and organized a group of gay men into a revolutionary association called the Society for Human Rights—at least, he tried to. There is, of course, a hidden story behind his efforts. Here it is.

WHO WAS HENRY GERBER

Henry Gerber was born Josef Henry Dittmar in Bavaria on June 29, 1892. He later changed his name to Henry Gerber. The young Josef immigrated to the United States with his parents in 1913, landing first at Ellis Island and then moving west to Chicago because of its large German Catholic population. He got a job working at the old Montgomery Ward and almost immediately found himself in trouble with the law—not because of any crime he had committed, or at least not anything he regarded as a crime.

Henry Gerber, né Josef Henry Dittmar, was gay. In Chicago, as in many other American cities in the 1920s, homosexuality was illegal. In 1917, when his sexual proclivities became known, he was committed to a mental institution, where he remained until the outbreak of World War I, at which point he was given a choice: enlist in the army or face internment. He chose the army.

Gerber was sent to Coblenz on the Rhine in Germany, where, as a printer and proofreader with the Allied Army of Occupation, he learned about Magnus Hirschfeld and the work he and his Scientific Humanitarian Committee were doing to reform anti-homosexual German law. He also traveled to Berlin, where he found a thriving gay subculture and a homophile magazine to which he subscribed. It was in Berlin that he had an epiphany—having witnessed what was happening in Germany, he would come back to the United States and advocate for similar change in American society, where homosexuals were persecuted because they deviated from established norms in sexual matters. "The United States is in a condition of chaos and misunderstanding concerning its sex laws," he wrote, "and no one is trying to unravel the tangle and bring relief to the abused."

He realized that the homosexual population needed nearly as much attention as the laws pertaining to their acts. In his opinion, too many homosexuals were ignorant about themselves and their preferences. They were "fearful, frantic, blasé, and even depraved—opting to search for forbidden fruit rather than pursue personal free expression." Unlike the prevalent thinking of the day (including among men with a homosexual orientation), Gerber did not believe that homosexuality was an illness, a psychiatric condition or unnatural. The question was how, in the face of these attitudes, could he bring about homosexual emancipation.

Open activity would bring him in conflict with law enforcement, and he would probably go to jail. He was not afraid of going to jail; he simply did not know how to fly in the face of such strongly entrenched opposition. Even the great Clarence Darrow had written that "no other offence has ever been visited with such severe penalties as seeking to bring help to the oppressed." His friends cautioned that a crusade to legitimize homosexuality would be both rash and futile. But the prospect of becoming known to history as the deliverer of the downtrodden— much like Lincoln, who emancipated the slaves—was irresistible. The homosexual population would benefit, and in the process, he, too, would benefit. No more mental institutions. No more fear of incarceration. No more clandestine meetings. Free and open expression of feelings and behavior loomed.

At this point, Gerber experienced his second "aha!" moment. He would create an organized society with legitimate goals and guidelines—a society that addressed the rights not just of homosexuals but also of all human beings. He would call this group the Society for Human Rights, an English translation of Hirschfeld's *Bund fur Menschenrect*, and he would incorporate a number of Hirschfeld's ideas about universal freedoms. With his direction clear, he drew up a set of goals and a working plan to execute those goals. Which brings us, finally, to Old Town, Crilly Court and its hidden gay history.

WALKING THE TALK ON CRILLY COURT

Gerber came back to Chicago from Germany in 1924. He got a job with the postal service and rented a room—not an apartment, as has been often written—in an old house at 1710 North Crilly Court. Why Crilly Court? Who knows. The row of Queen Anne–style houses had fallen on hard times after the First World War. Two operated openly as brothels. Others had been repossessed by banks and had become tenements whose landladies sat barefoot on the steps and threw bones to dogs in the tiny front yards. Gerber moved into one of the "tenements." It was here, in December 1924, that he organized the Society for Human Rights (SHR) and filed an application for a charter as a nonprofit organization with the State of Illinois, listing himself as secretary. An African American clergyman named John T. Graves signed on as president of the group. Gerber and five others were listed as directors.

The state granted the charter on December 10, 1924, making the society the oldest documented homosexual organization in the nation. The society promised to

> *promote the interests of people, who by reasons of mental and physical abnormalities, are abused and hindered in the legal pursuit of happiness which is guaranteed them by the Declaration of Independence and to combat the public prejudices against them by dissemination of factors according to modern science among intellectuals of mature age. The Society stands only for law and order; it is in harmony with any and all general laws insofar as they protect*

the rights of others, and does in no manner recommend any acts in violation of present laws nor advocate any manner inimical to the public welfare.

Because the goals were deliberately vague, and homosexuality was not mentioned in the mission statement, Gerber felt that if the mission of the society was one of human rights, the organization would be more likely to gain public acceptance and be less controversial. No one with the state investigated any further before issuing the charter.

Gerber was not happy with the makeup of his group. He had hoped to get both financial and personal backing from professional men in Chicago's homosexual community, especially medical authorities and sex education advocates. He believed these men, who had been forced to meet secretly in theaters and gay bars on the north side, would welcome the opportunity to be part of a reputable organization of like-minded individuals. But when, as secretary of the new organization, he wrote soliciting support, the professionals ignored him. Given the misconception on the part of the general public about the nature of homosexuality, prominent gays did not want to be persecuted for this misconception. Associating with the society could tarnish their reputations, ruin their livelihoods and cause them to be disowned by their families. Also, it would have been common for many such individuals to marry and have families, given the significant social and familial pressure to do so, while still being attracted to men. A further problem was that homosexuals at that time did not "organize." They were so fearful of being "outed" that they did not get together openly. Most felt that as long as some homosexual sex acts were against the law, they should not let their names be used as part of any homosexual organization.

The only support Gerber got was from poor people. John, the president of the organization, was a black minister who earned his living by preaching to small groups of African Americans about brotherly love. Al, a director, was an indigent "laundry queen," a military term given to men who did laundry as opposed to more manly duties. Ralph, also a director, worked for the railroad and was in constant fear of losing his job should his nature become known. Not an auspicious beginning, and in Gerber's opinion, "dead wrong." But he had no other choice.

Shortly after the society's incorporation, Gerber started a newsletter, *Friendship and Freedom*. This was a very important publication since it was the first gay-interest publication in the United States. In it, he outlined a three-point strategy for winning homosexual emancipation:

Engage in a series of lectures pointing out the attitude of society in relation to their own behavior and especially urging against the seduction of adolescents.

Through a publication, keep the homophile world in touch with the progress of our efforts.

Through self-discipline, win the confidence and assistance of legal authorities and legislators in understanding the problem: that these authorities should be educated on the futility and folly of long prison terms for those committing homosexual acts.

The first issue of *Friendship and Freedom* was written in the basement of the Crilly Court house. The second may, or may not, have been. Unfortunately, only two issues of the newsletter were ever printed, and neither is still in existence. Gerber wrote and financed publication of both issues, but he was disheartened to find that few homosexuals, including SHR members themselves, were even willing to receive the newsletter, fearing that postal inspectors would consider the publication obscene. Under the Comstock Act of 1783, the brainchild of a zealous New England Congregationalist, dissemination of any "article of an immoral nature" was prohibited and punishable by arrest and incarceration. All gay-interest publications were considered immoral until 1958, when the Supreme Court ruled that publishing homosexual content did not mean the content was automatically obscene. In 1924, postal censors cooperated with local law enforcement agencies to identify and punish sex deviants.

For a year, the tiny group met and planned in Old Town. They decided to concentrate their efforts on the state of Illinois and to focus on reform of those laws criminalizing homosexual acts. Gerber and John Graves agreed to make SHR a purely homophile organization, excluding the much larger circle of bisexuals. Neither knew at the time that Al Weininger, their vice-president, was bisexual and that he had a wife and two small children.

OUT OF THE 'HOOD

For whatever reason, Gerber decided to move from Crilly Court to "Towertown" in 1925. It was not a good move. Whereas he was able to operate in relative obscurity in Old Town, he was far more visible closer to Chicago's Loop. One Sunday morning, about 2:00 a.m., Gerber returned from a visit downtown. Shortly after he entered his room, there was a knock on the door. Thinking it might be his landlady, he opened it. Two men entered and identified themselves as a city detective and a newspaper reporter from the *Examiner*. The detective asked where the boy was. "What boy?" asked Gerber. Of course, there was no boy, but the detective informed Gerber that he had orders from his precinct captain to arrest and take him to the police station for indecent behavior. He took Gerber's typewriter, his notary public diploma, all of the SHR literature, personal diaries and bookkeeping accounts. At no time did he show a warrant for the arrest and confiscation of property.

At the police station, Gerber was locked up in a cell, but no charges were made against him. He stayed in lockup through the night. The next morning, he was given permission to call his boss, to explain that he would not be coming in for a short time. The boss tried to save his job by writing down that he was "absent on leave." After the call, Gerber was taken to the Chicago Avenue Police Court. There, he found John the preacher, Al the laundry queen and a young man who happened to be with Al at the time of the arrest. No one knew what had happened to bring about their arrests. Finally, a friendly cop showed them a copy of the *Examiner*. There, on the front page, was an incredible headline and story: "Strange Sex Cult Exposed."

The article said that Al was in the practice of bringing male friends to his home and, in full view of his wife and children, performing "strange sex acts" with them, causing Al's wife to call a social worker in the summer of 1925. The social worker then reported the "strange doings" of these "degenerates" to the police. The article went on to say that when the police raided Al's apartment, they found John the preacher, Henry the postal employee and a young man. They arrested all of them. Among the effects in the apartment, they reported to have retrieved a pamphlet that urged men to leave their wives and children.

Gerber denied the article as out-and-out untruth and a perversion of the facts. In fact, John was alone in his apartment at the time of the arrest, as was Gerber. Neither was with Al, whom they did not even know was married. The entire incident was unconscionable since no warrants had been obtained for their arrests. (Gerber speculated that the police had probably expected to find them in bed since they could not imagine homosexuals any other way.) Property had been illegally confiscated and constitutional rights violated.

Al confided to Gerber that he had confessed to the sin of homosexuality but said that he had not supplied the information contained in the article.

On Monday after the arrest, the arresting detective produced a powder puff, reportedly found in Gerber's room, which he claimed to be evidence of his effeminacy. That was the sole evidence offered to the judge attesting to Gerber's "crime." At the trial, the social worker read out of context from his diary, "I love Karl"—further proof of Gerber's degeneracy. Both the detective and the judge expressed outrage at such depravity. The evidence convinced an already prejudiced court. At the conclusion of the first trial—there would be two others—all men were found guilty by reason of homosexuality.

Gerber, John and Al were sent to separate cells in the Cook County Jail after the trial ended. A young Jew, with whom Gerber was incarcerated, asked if he wanted a lawyer and recommended a friend who practiced in the criminal courts. Gerber accepted the offer and met with the attorney, whom he later declared a "shyster." But the shyster did know his way around the criminal courts and had a reputation for making a good living by taking on doubtful cases. The lawyer promised to get Gerber out on bail and to get him a second trial for a fee of $200.

The second trial of the "deviant three" began on the following Thursday—before the same judge. Also present were two postal inspectors, who threatened to see to it that the men got heavy prison sentences for "infecting God's own country." The attorney immediately asked for a mistrial on the grounds that there was insufficient evidence to hold the men. The judge ordered the attorney to shut up or be held in contempt. The postal inspectors said that the federal commissioner would take the case under advisement from the obscenity angle. After much haggling, the judge agreed to set bail for the defendants at $1,000 each. The lawyer made the arrangements and collected his fee.

After being released on bail, Gerber reported for work at the post office but was told that he had been suspended based on the testimony of the postal inspectors. He would have to await the findings of the federal commissioner. He then went to see the editor of the *Examiner*, citing all the lies and misinformation contained in the article. The editor promised to look into the matter. He never did.

A friend obtained a better lawyer for the three who, for another $200, promised a third trial and a fair shake. True to his word, the new lawyer arranged matters. On the day of the trial, the three appeared before a new presiding judge. Also present in the court were the arresting detective, the post office inspectors and even the first lawyer, who had become very interested in the case. The social worker chose not to attend. The new judge, who had reviewed the earlier trials, reprimanded the prosecution. "It is an outrage to arrest persons without a warrant," he decreed. "I order the case dismissed." Because Al had pleaded guilty to disorderly conduct, he received a fine of $10 and costs. Neither Gerber nor John was fined.

The attorney told the judge that the commissioner would take no action on the obscenity charge in the matter of mailed literature. The judge then ordered the detective to return Gerber's property. He got back the typewriter but not the diaries, which had been turned over to the postal inspectors. But Gerber had learned a valuable lesson. He never put anything remotely incriminating in his diaries again.

The experience convinced Gerber, if he hadn't been convinced before, that he and his friends were up against a solid wall of ignorance, hypocrisy, meanness and corruption, and the wall had won. Even after the case was dismissed, the detective issued a parting shot: "What was the idea of the Society for Human Rights anyway? Was it to give you birds the legal right to rape every boy on the street?" The lawyer told Gerber he could probably be reinstated with the post office, but he was in no mood to pursue it. He had no more money to fight the organization. A few weeks later, he received an official letter from Washington stating that he had been dismissed from the Post Office Department for conduct unbecoming a postal worker. That was the end of the Society for Human Rights.

The End of It All

Good-bye to all that.
—Robert Graves

In 1927, Henry Gerber left Chicago for good. He went to New York, where a friend from his army days introduced him to a colonel who had seen service in the war. The colonel encouraged Gerber to reenlist, which he did. The army did not delve into its recruits' sexual histories back then, so Gerber was able to serve until 1945, when he received an honorable discharge and a pension of $100 per month. During his second enlistment, he ran a pen pal service called "Connections," which had about two hundred members, mostly heterosexual. He also wrote on gay matters for a variety of magazines under a pseudonym, Parisex, as well as his own name. His contributions to *ONE* magazine are noteworthy. *ONE*, which came out of the Mattachine Society in the 1950s, won an important First Amendment case before the U.S. Supreme Court involving the United States Post Office and materials declared obscene. The Mattachine Society was the first gay civil rights organization formed after the Society for Human Rights, and *ONE* magazine may have been the first gay periodical after *Friendship and Freedom*—some thirty years later.

When he left the army for a second time, Gerber returned to New York and became part of the gay scene there. He carried on correspondence with other gay men, even going so far as to discuss gay organizing and strategies for addressing societal prejudice. Near the end of his life, he moved to the Soldiers' and Airmens' Home in Washington, D.C., where he worked on his memoirs and translations of German novels. He died in the home on December 31, 1972, at the age of eighty.

A Legacy

So what can we make of Henry Gerber, the crotchety Bavarian godfather of the modern gay rights movement in the United States? He was, and is, a very complex man—passionate about the idea of human rights and individual self-expression but very different from other homosexuals of his time. Neither a drinker nor a smoker, he did not socialize with other gays in speakeasies. A very masculine type, he did not like to associate with effeminate men ("queens") or older homosexual men. He was immune to female charms, though he said he did not hate women. He did not approve of lesbians and refused to associate with them. He was an introvert who enjoyed music and reading (mostly nonfiction). Though he was brought up Catholic, he renounced religion as a racket, saying that God loves atheists because they don't "molest him with silly prayers." He was not interested in smut or obscenity and considered himself very civilized and self-sufficient. As for his sexual liaisons, he was mostly interested in young boys and quick anonymous sex in theaters. He suffered periodic beatings, theft and blackmail. He was constantly being harassed, but never intimidated, by postal snoops. At great personal risk, he wrote and published a paper in 1934 denouncing Hitler's persecution of homosexuals and his (Hitler's) murder of storm trooper chief of staff Ernst Roehm and other storm troopers. A most unusual man.

As for his legacy, Henry Gerber was a brave man who fought bigotry at a time in our history when it was extremely dangerous to do so. He founded the first gay civil rights organization in the United States in an effort to promote and protect the interests of people who, by reasons of mental and physical abnormalities, are abused and hindered in the legal pursuit of happiness, guaranteed by the Declaration of Independence. He serves as a direct link between the homophile-related activism of the Weimar Republic and the American homophile movement of the 1950s. And he founded the nation's first gay-interest publication.

But that is not the end of his story. In 1992, Gerber was made a local hero when he was posthumously inducted into the Gay and Lesbian Hall of Fame for all of his achievements on behalf of homosexuals. And in 2000, Chicago singled out Gerber for an honor beyond what the city had, to that time, showered on far more famous residents such as Carl Sandburg, Muddy Waters or Walt Disney. The Commission on Landmarks recommended that

A plaque commemorating the founding of the Society for Human Rights by Henry Gerber. *Photo by Norman Baugher.*

Gerber's former residence at 1710 North Crilly Court, a modest two-and-a-half-story row house, be given landmark status. In doing so, landmark officials said they were well aware that they might have opened a complex debate. Exactly what criteria should be used when deeming someone's house a historical landmark? Did Gerber's work to promote homosexual rights deserve such recognition?

They had a long discussion before taking the proposal to the city council, including getting support from the home's current owners. Members of the commission did the research and concluded that Gerber's residence qualified. The council agreed, and on June 1, 2001, the house was designated a Chicago landmark.

One wonders what Henry Gerber would have thought of this posthumous recognition. He would probably have been pleased, given his desire to go down in history as an emancipator of the downtrodden. He has been recognized as just that.

8

TELEPHONES, TECHNOLOGY AND THE SHADY LADIES OF OLD TOWN

Even the most painstaking history is a bridge across an eternal mystery.
—*Bruce Catton*

D eep in the pages of Old Town's hidden history is a relatively unknown individual—unknown to the general public, that is, but famous among his peers and contemporaries. He was an accidental inventor who stumbled into an industry at its inception, began at the bottom of the ladder during its formative years and made his way to the top. At the end of his life's journey, he had left a significant and lasting impact on American life.

TINKER, TAILOR, TELEPHONE MAKER: JOSEPH J. O'CONNELL, 1861–1956

Joseph O'Connell came to Old Town in a house. Literally. In the mid-nineteenth century, his family lived in what is now known as the North Loop—just off Pine Street (Michigan Avenue). Bartholomew, his father, decided he wanted to move farther north—to a less settled area of the city. But he didn't do what most people who wanted to relocate would do—sell his house and build or buy another one. He moved his house. House moving was actually fairly common at that time. A house was raised up off its original foundation—this was usually done with the use of screw jacks. Sections of the foundation were removed to allow placement of the screw jacks under the sills. The house was then put on a sled-like contraption and hauled, or placed on rollers and pulled. The rollers moved over heavy wooden timbers placed beneath the raised building. Animal power accomplished the rest. By means of a rope and pulley, a team of two animals pulled the building over the timbers. As the house moved forward, the timbers from behind were taken up and replaced ahead of it. As long as the move was well managed, the interior plaster would remain uncracked. What is unusual about the O'Connell situation is that the family actually lived in the house while it was being moved. They treated the experience as though it were a big picnic. They stood outside and waved to people they passed, ate, sang and had a wonderful time.

Home of Joseph O'Connell, inventor of twenty-nine devices that made possible the modern telephone. *Photo by Carolyn Blackmon.*

They were on the road for three days. They traveled west from Rush and Chestnut Streets to State Street and then turned north. They rode over a sand road to reach their destination—the Cabbage Patch. On the way, they passed three historic old breweries: the Eagle, the Brand and the Lill-Diversey, the latter owned by Michael Diversey, who had donated land for the building of St. Michael's Church. Finally, they arrived at 407 West Eugenie, where they unloaded the house. While we don't know what this house looked like—it was destroyed in the Great Fire of 1871— we can guess that it was a simple, balloon-frame structure, large enough to accommodate the O'Connell family.

The house was reduced to ashes in the Great Fire. Bartholomew, like many of his neighbors, received aid from the Chicago Fire and Aid Society, which he used to rebuild the new house on the site of the old in 1872. The first house was made entirely of wood. It was later raised, and a brick ground floor was added, along with a twenty-four-foot addition to the front. A second residence was built on the site in 1885 by Bartholomew's son, Joseph. Since wood construction had been outlawed in 1874, this house probably had aluminum siding with wood Italianate detail.

The houses stayed in the possession of the O'Connells until 1978, when they were sold to Terry G. Dysert, who made extensive changes. He added a garage, a patio, a new porch and a first-story entrance. On the west side, Dysert placed a second-story porch room with glass doors. A brick rear section completed the additions. The original structure looks much like its Eugenie Street neighbors. The garage and second-story porch have a more European feel. One neighbor likened the house to the compounds in the hill villages of southern France. But Joseph would have had no way of knowing this, since he did not see the finished structures.

JOSEPH J. O'CONNELL: THE STORY

The tale of the residences at 405–07 West Eugenie is interesting, but it pales in comparison to that of the life of Joseph J. O'Connell, a man who was the epitome of the American success story. He was a brilliant electrical engineer and inventor whose humble beginnings gave no indication of the niche he would carve for himself in American history. Joseph was born in Chicago in 1861 to a working-class family. He attended St. Joseph's School, the School of the Immaculate Conception and the Newberry School. He left school in 1878 and in September became a goldbeater for George Reeves in the Lakeside Building at Clark and Adams Streets. He spent his days pounding the metal into thin sheets that could be used to encase or cover objects, giving them the appearance of solid gold. For this work, he earned $2.50 a week. He later said that he couldn't stand the prosperity of the job, so he quit, and in October 1878, he went to work as a messenger for the American District Telegraph Company for $17.00 a month—the first of his steps up the economic ladder in the industry to which he would make invaluable contributions. Telegraph lines, up to the time of the telephone, had provided the only means of electrical communication, and many of the men active in the operation of the telegraph were the first to become agents, promoters, constructors and inventors who introduced and developed the telephone. They were the pioneers and brought to the task the experience of many years in the telegraph service.

Joseph's did not remain a messenger for long. Within a month, he was printing tickets, billheads and envelopes. The next year, in early June 1879, he became a telegraph repairman for which he was paid a whopping $40.00 per month. He did so well as a repairman that by June 1882, he was able to afford himself a few luxuries. He went shopping on Chicago's famous shopping mecca, State Street, and bought a gold watch and chain for $35.25 from the firm of W.B. Clapp Brothers, which was located on the corner of State and Monroe. But the best was yet to come. By the end of June, he was supervising two offices and received a $2.00-a-day pay increase. This enabled him to go on a real buying spree. He purchased a rifle for $3.00, a suit of clothes for $24.00, a hat for $2.00 and a necktie for $1.00. We can only assume that his new position required him to dress more formally.

He went from repairman to putting in signal boxes for the fast-developing telephone industry at a salary of $2.25 per hour. He installed boxes in Lyon and Healy's Music Store and in the Sibley Hiram Seed House on Randolph Street. The experience with Lyon and Healy was an interesting one. The store opened in Chicago in 1864 as a sheet music shop. Only six days after the opening, they ran their first advertisement in the *Chicago Tribune*. It appeared next to the account of General Sherman's march from Atlanta to the sea. The music store's owners were so successful that they expanded into the manufacture and sales of musical instruments. Seven years later, they were one of the few businesses to survive the economic depression after the Great Fire because they had purchased enough insurance to allow them to rebuild. Once the rebuilding was complete, Healy developed a new merchandising tool: a picture book or illustrated catalogue that went against the secret price sales and sales-from-samples tradition of that era.

Of course, such an enterprising company would be one of the first to have a telephone signal box installed, and as luck would have it, Joseph O'Connell was the installer. Because of this association, Joseph developed a lifelong love of music. He bought one of the company's first manufactured violins for $2.50, a violin case for $1.50 and a bow for $2.50. He even purchased a series of music lessons, for which he paid $5.00 in advance.

In July 1883, there was trouble at the telephone company. The linemen protested the company's new policy of having workers pay for their own uniforms. The men thought the company should pay, or at least give them a raise to cover the cost of the clothing. The company refused, and the men formed a union that became known as the Brotherhood of Telegraphers. They went on strike, but they did not stop work immediately. The company's officers refused to negotiate with the strikers as a group, although they did agree to arbitrate individual cases. Fifty linemen walked off the job and demanded a 25 percent pay raise. Joseph O'Connell did not join the strikers. For his loyalty, he was rewarded with a pay increase to $75.00 a month. The strikers did not fare so well.

Inventions and promotions followed in quick succession. In 1880, O'Connell designed and installed the first common battery system in connection with operators' telephones in the Chicago Main Office. It was one of the most important inventions of the time. In August 1884, he was made chief inspector of the Chicago Telephone Company. In 1886, he installed an electric lamp as a signal in a burglar alarm office operated by the telephone company. This was probably the first signal of its kind operated by a relay controlled over a wire from a distant point. Between 1887 and 1906, he applied for and received twenty-nine patents relating to electrical apparatus for the telephone system. From 1893 to 1911, the telephone business in Chicago developed so rapidly that investment in buildings, subways, switchboards, cables and telephone plants soared, increasing the company's worth from $3 million in 1893 to more than $30 million in 1911. The number of telephones increased from 10,000 to more than 300,000, bearing out Thomas Edison's observation that "someone working for Bell Telephone should stick with it because it is a very good business, indeed."

Joseph O'Connell's telephone inventions improved the switchboards and signaling devices and solved many fundamental problems of the new service. One of his main contributions was a phantom circuit in which two pairs of wires carried three messages, a forerunner of the later carrier systems. O'Connell considered this his finest piece of work. In 1889, he experimented with the metallic circuit, whereby it was possible to carry on a double conversation over a circuit without interference of one conversation with another. Shortly thereafter, he designed and put into service a common battery system, which made possible the operation of all telephones used by the operators of a telephone exchange. Previous to this, each telephone had an individual battery. In 1902, he invented the coin collector for telephone lines. He had come a long way from his goldbeating days.

A MAN FOR ALL SEASONS

Joseph O'Connell lived to be ninety-five years old. In the course of his long and eventful life, Joseph married and had four children. All of them became teachers. He worked for the Chicago Phone Company, later to become the Illinois Bell Telephone Company, for fifty years before he retired in 1930. After retirement, he spent his days working on the Eugenie Street house and playing with his grandchildren. He installed a rope swing on the upstairs porch for the children, which they loved. They would swing very high trying to touch the tapestries that hung on the walls of the porch. On very hot days, Joseph filled tubs with ice purchased from the icehouse on North Avenue and placed an electric fan next to them to send out cool air. Other days, they played baseball in the backyard. On Saturday afternoons in the summer, Joseph would take them to the Plaza Theater, partly for their entertainment and partly so he could cool off. Usually, he fell asleep during the feature, and the children were able to watch Tom Mix ride to the rescue of a damsel in distress twice.

O'Connell's memories spanned two centuries. He remembered sitting on his father's shoulders in 1865, watching the funeral procession for Abraham Lincoln when the train bearing the president's body stopped in Chicago. During the mourning period for Lincoln, the O'Connells draped their Rush Street house in black. They had to use dress material because cotton was hard to get during the Civil War. When the bunting was taken down, Joseph's frugal grandmother made a dress from the material.

He had a vivid memory of the Great Fire of 1871. Many family friends from the North Loop had brought their furniture to the O'Connells' front yard in the mistaken belief that the fire would not spread north of the Chicago River. It did, and the families lost everything. Joseph recalled spending the night of the fire on the open prairie under blankets suspended between barrels.

He witnessed the birth of some of the most important inventions and events of the modern era—some of which he himself brought into being: the telephone, the automobile, the radio, the phonograph, the computer, the motion picture, television, atomic energy and two world wars. His lifetime spanned the administrations of twenty presidents. He was so valued by the company to which he had devoted his life and creative energies that, in 1979, the Illinois Bell Telephone Company installed a handsome two- by three-foot bronze plaque on the front of his Eugenie house. The plaque commemorated Mr. O'Connell's long years of service and his many contributions to the telephone industry.

CALL ME MADAM: JOSEPH J. O'CONNELL AND THE SHADY LADIES OF CRILLY COURT

A short three-block stroll and a lifestyle away, two houses on Crilly Court had been making "good" use of Mr. O'Connell's inventions. Public officials and many private citizens in Chicago viewed prostitution as a necessary evil and tried to segregate it into a few poor neighborhoods to protect the rest of Chicago. Pockets of vice formed as early as the 1850s. Although the notorious lakefront brothel district, called the Sands, was destroyed by city officials in 1857, prostitution continued to thrive and expand on the near west side and the near north side. Intermittent raids on the "houses" through the late nineteenth and early twentieth centuries were aimed not at closing the brothels but at maintaining a flow of bribes to police, politicians and politically connected crime bosses. Raids also helped preserve public order within the districts and control their borders.

Vice was spreading throughout Chicago into "call house" flats and other covert locations. These depended on a communications network of pimps, taxi drivers and saloonkeepers. The automobile and the telephone helped free prostitution from geographic limits.

From 1910 through the 1920s, prostitution flourished on the near north side, especially the area around Clark Street and Chicago Avenue and as far north as Old Town. Two houses on Crilly Court attracted a large number of clients, thanks to the telephone system and cooperative cabbies—as Alexander and Kappy Maley discovered, to their chagrin. Alexander and

Crilly Court, the site of two well-known Chicago brothels in the 1920s and 1930s.
Photo by Carolyn Blackmon.

Kappy signed a lease on the house at 1716 North Crilly Court in 1937. The once-stately row of Queen Anne houses had fallen on hard times after World War I and during the Great Depression. Despite its sad state of disrepair, the Maleys fell in love with the place, but they did wonder what sort of people had lived there before. There were pay phones scattered all over the house and partitions installed to create many small rooms. The houses on either side of 1716 were rather shabby rooming houses and not very inviting. Edgar Crilly, son of Daniel Crilly, the original developer, was managing the houses. He was anxious to bring the court back to his father's plan: a street occupied by young married couples and entertainment professionals. He tore down the partitions, removed the phones, put in a second bathroom, installed carpeting and had the house painted. For this, the Maleys agreed to pay fifty dollars per month in rent.

In the meantime, Irma O'Toole (née Koenigsberg, daughter of the popular Wells Street saloonkeeper) had actually purchased the house at 1706 from the Crillys, which influenced the decision of the Maleys to move in. The O'Tooles had done extensive renovations on their property and planted a lovely back garden. Next to the O'Tooles, 1704 was still a rental, but it had a cared-for appearance and clean windows. Kappy dropped by there one afternoon hoping to get some decorating tips for 1716. She was courteously received by a handsome older lady and a beautiful young one. During the course of her visit, several other young women came into the room in something hardly considered daytime attire. As was the case with her own place, Kappy observed several small rooms divided by partitions and telephones, which kept ringing. It was then that Kappy realized where she was. She had wandered into one of Chicago's infamous "call houses." The older woman was the madam; the younger ones were her "girls." The calls were from prospective clients. Kappy said her hurried goodbyes and left. It is uncertain what, if any, decorating tips she came away with.

The real surprise came a week after the Maleys had moved into their house at 1716. One morning, at three o'clock, they were awakened by a loud knocking at the front door. Alexander, groggy from being roused at such an hour, opened the upstairs window. "Who is it, and what do you want?" he asked, half thinking that his friends were playing a prank on them.

There, at the front door, stood a cabdriver. "Is the madam in?" asked the cabbie.

"Yes," replied Alexander, "but she's in bed."

Telephones, Technology and the Shady Ladies of Old Town

The cabbie went back and relayed the message to three disappointed passengers in his vehicle who directed him to drive on. At that point, the Maleys realized that they, too, had moved into a "whorehouse," which some thought was still operating. The partitions they had seen when they walked through the house had obviously been installed to allow more room for entertaining guests. The phones were there to take appointments.

Though the Maleys tried to straighten things out with the vice squad, cabbies were still directed to Crilly Court by lecherous patrons for many years afterward. Prostitution was a lucrative business in Chicago, often run by the mob and protected by unscrupulous politicians.

9

LEO WEISSENBORN, 1877–1967

Just an Ordinary (Old Town) Man

A morsel of genuine history is a thing so rare as to be always valuable.
—*Thomas Jefferson*

Mid pleasures and palaces though we may roam,
Be it ever so humble there's no place like home.
—*Henry Rowley Bishop, 1823*

W̶ho is Leo J. Weissenborn, you might wonder, and why should he be part of Old Town's hidden history? If you try to Google him, and if you are very persistent, you will find a couple of things—namely, that he was born in Sauk City, Wisconsin, in 1877; that he moved to Old Town in 1886; that he was educated in Chicago; and that he went on to become a prominent architect, one of the designers responsible for the Chicago Tribune Tower and the addition housing the WGN radio station. He also designed the pedestal for the famous Nathan Hale statue located in the plaza north of the Tribune Tower. All of this is interesting but not necessarily enough to put him in the Old Town Hall of Fame.

Fortunately, we know a good deal more about Leo Weissenborn than the bare-bones information on Google. We know this because, at age seventy-eight, Leo wrote his recollections of an Old Town boyhood and left the unpublished manuscript to the Chicago History Museum. He later synopsized his musings for the 1955 Old Town Art Fair program book, which he called, *Here Is Old Town Past*. Both provide a firsthand account of Old Town life at the end of the nineteenth century and what it was like growing up there.

Hudson Avenue Days, 1886

The Weissenborn family moved to Old Town in 1886, when Leo was just nine years old. Their first address was 1933 North Hudson, near Wisconsin Street. From the day he arrived, young Leo was taken with his surroundings, so much so that they stayed with him during a very long and productive life. Let's start with his earliest memories of the look of Old Town, circa 1886. He tells us that the streets were paved with cedar blocks and surfaced with tar and gravel—as were streets throughout Chicago at the time. Signs on the streetlamps identified his block as Church Street (which Hudson was called at that time). Looking down the block and across the way, there were some landmarks that stood out in the old man's memory. Where Ogden Avenue intersected with North Clark Street, there was a distinctive, flat iron–shaped, three-story brick building bounded by Clark Street, Center Street (now Armitage Avenue) and Wisconsin. A Masonic Lodge Hall occupied the top floor of this building, where the Chicago Ethical Culture Society held its Sunday school classes. (The building has long since been torn down.)

That building led to Lincoln Park, which figured prominently in Weissenborn's early years. Garfield Avenue (now called Dickens) was considered the main entry to Lincoln Park. Picture this—at this Garfield entry stood a bronze sphinx mounted on granite blocks, a gift of the map publisher Andrew McNally, who came to the neighborhood after the Great Fire. That sphinx was a prime target for Leo and his friends. Every Halloween night, the neighborhood boys would gather and paint the breast of the statue bright red. And every year, the city would dispatch workers to come out and clean it up. One Halloween, Leo remembers, the boys got really creative. First, they painted the breast of the sphinx red, and then they covered it with huge whalebone corsets. That was the last straw. The Park District authorities hauled the sphinx away. No worries—the boys found other diversions, as you will see.

In the summer of 1886, the North Pond in Lincoln Park was excavated, and the dirt was scooped up into a mound between the pond and Lake Shore Drive. That winter was very cold and snowy, much like the infamous winter of 2011, and the mound was covered with ice and snow. As the winter wore on, the mound grew higher and more slippery. Boys being boys, Weissenborn and his friends took advantage of the temporary "mountain." They carried their sleds to the top of the frozen heap and, at risk of life and limb, raced them down to the bottom and across the frozen pond. This was another aggravation for the Park District. Fortunately, the ice held, and no one drowned. Unfortunately for Leo, the exertions were too much. He became overheated, caught a cold, contracted pneumonia and was forced to stay home for a month—effectively ending his tobogganing career.

Never at a loss for mischief, Leo and his Old Town pals found yet another way to aggravate city officials. At century's end, horse-drawn carriages still operated on Wells Street, but they were slowly being replaced by cable cars. With the advent of cable cars, Leo and his friends took themselves over to the tracks with bags full of tin cans, which they tied to a rope. They proceeded to dangle the rope down the slot between the cable car tracks until it became tangled with the cable. They stood by laughing hysterically as the cars noisily made their way downtown, dragging the cans along the tracks.

A MOVE TO 1713 NORTH WELLS

From Hudson, the Weissenborns moved to the second floor of a large, two-story brick house at 1713 North Wells Street. It was a new venue—with a new set of sights and adventures. The first floor was occupied by a kindergarten and primary school, which was attended by children of well-to-do German families living on LaSalle and Dearborn Streets. In the late 1800s, Old Town was still predominately German, although a good many other ethnic groups had moved in. At the rear of the Wells Street house was a playground with gym equipment, where many of the neighborhood children gathered to play. The grounds also included a vegetable garden, later the site of the Georgian Apartments, and a large empty lot that gave Leo a direct view into his beloved Lincoln Park. From his rear window, he could look out on the last remnants of the old City Cemetery—on the north, the boulder marking the grave of David Kennison, widely believed at that time to be the last survivor of the Boston Tea Party (we now know better), and to the south, the imposing Couch Mausoleum.

Just north of 1713 North Wells was another empty lot where the kids played fort and built huge dugouts until it was taken over by the prestigious German social and athletic club, Turn Gemeinde. The Chicago Turn dated back to the Civil War, when it was located on North Clark Street. In 1861, it proudly sent off a regiment to fight for the preservation of the Union. The club remained at the North Clark Street for many years, but when that facility could no longer accommodate their increased activities, they

Leo Weissenborn, 1877–1967

An old Chicago streetcar, Eugenie and Wells, 1940. *Photographer unknown.*

constructed a new building on the east side of Wells Street and St. Paul next to the Weissenborns. The new facility was a lively place and the scene of a lot of Old Town activity. It housed a gymnasium, a billiard room, a library, a social club, a dining room, a dance hall and a theater for stage productions and political debates. By the early twentieth century, many of the old German families started to leave Old Town, and members of the Turn Gemeinde migrated north. They relocated their club to Lincoln Avenue and Montrose. The Wells Street building was then taken over by the Skiget-Wright Photographic Studio and later Dallas and Jones Productions. An Old Town showplace in the late nineteenth and early twentieth centuries, the building, like so many other historic places, has been torn down.

During the last winter of the Weissenborn's stay on Wells Street, the youngest son contracted diphtheria, and the older children were sent to stay with various friends and relatives. Mr. Weissenborn also came down with the disease and had to be confined in the Alexian Brothers Hospital on Orleans Street, just south of North Avenue. As an aside (and Weissenborn's memoirs had many asides), the Alexian brothers sold the property to permit the proposed elevated railroad to make the bend into the alley south of North Avenue. A new Alexian Brothers Hospital was then built on Belden Avenue.

ON TO WEST NORTH AVENUE

For whatever reason, Weissenborn wrote that "it was found incompatible for a family to live under the same roof with a school," so the family moved yet again to the second floor of a building at 413 West North Avenue. Here, he described a deck built over a barn on the alley line that was used for hanging up laundry and for the kids to play. Leo and his siblings would stand at the alley railing and try to visualize the proposed elevated train passing by, although this did not happen until a decade later, after the Weissenborns had moved on.

The North Avenue deck had other compensations for the young boy. Life on North Avenue was marked by a series of parades. He could stand on the deck and watch the annual Labor Day parade complete with floats, bands and dignitaries pass by on the way to a big picnic at Ogden's Grove near Clybourne Avenue. There were also circus parades and a Knights of Columbus Parade to capture their attention. During election times, there were political parades replete with banners, slogans and bands. The marchers wore colorful capes and caps and carried torches, a spectacle, according to Weissenborn, "now gone into oblivion." When it was too cold for parades, the family looked out the window and saw "jolly maskaraders on their way to Muellers Hall at Sedgwick Street."

Northwest corner of North Avenue and Wells, a popular street in Old Town during the days of streetcar transportation. *Photo by Charley Hughes.*

A parade in Old Town, Eugenie, Clark and LaSalle Streets. Performance by General George Bell Jr., Post 150, 1939–41, VFW Band. *ICHI 26953. Photographer unknown.*

Mr. Edelman, the organist at St. Michael's Church and a member of the Old Thomas Orchestra, occupied the flat to the left of the Weissenborns on North Avenue. Of Edelman, Leo recalled, "His colleagues once brought him a Seranade before the hour of midnight. I don't recall the occasion for same; however we kids were frightened when awakened from a sound sleep by their music."

A SHORT STAY ON EUGENIE

From North Avenue, the traveling Weissenborns moved to 323 West Eugenie Street, to the first floor of a two-story red brick house built in 1882 and now classified as "architecturally significant" on the National Register of Historic Places. The rectangular-shaped house had a three-bay front façade with limestone banding, a flat roof and an ornamental cornice with brackets. Visitors to Old Town can still walk by and see the house with all these original features. Next door, at 321, was a frame house built in 1874, just before the city outlawed frame construction within the city limits. According to Leo, this was then one of the best buildings in the neighborhood. The previous occupants of the flat were the family of Louis Nettlehorst, who for many years was president of the Chicago Board of Education. Nettlehorst had a school on Broadway named for him. Frieda and Carl Nettlehorst were in Leo's class at LaSalle School.

Leo recalled that "while living on Eugenie Street, we watched the construction of the Bowling Alley, now the Menomonee Boys Club, at the corner of Menomonee and Willow Streets—then named Tell Court—as well as the St. Jacob Kirche, now St. James Church on Orleans Street facing North Park Avenue, whose pastor was Dr. Zimmerman, then supervisor of German in Chicago schools. This recalls other [German] residents of this locality, such as Gabrial Katzenberger, supervisor of singing; and Herman Haustein, supervisor of drawing; both of the Chicago High Schools."

LaSalle School Days

Leo's elementary school days were a special time. In his memoir, he recalled

>*periodic sallies into the classroom of our principal, Homer Bevens, who would read to the class chapters from John Burroughs* Wake Robin *or Henry Thoreau's* Walden Pond. *Principal Bevens also conducted the singing in the eighth grade. Thus, when we put on a Cantata on my graduation in 1892, it was at the Windsor Theatre on North Clark Street, as the LaSalle School then only had its eighth grade room enlarged by the addition of the former cloak room space to serve as an auditorium. The eighth grade students then had to share the seventh grade cloak room. At this time, a collection was taken up among the higher grade students and a Sohmer Piano purchased, which may still be functioning in the school.* [It is not.]*

>   *After my graduation, the corner addition to LaSalle School was built which provided an auditorium on the top floor, but the building took away the play yard. The neighborhood children then played on Eugenie Street; and in inclement weather, sallied down Eugenie Street to Set. Michael's Church, wherein they played tag and hide-go-seek among the pews and in the*

LaSalle School, 1950. *ICHI 26843. Photo by Harold S. Beach.*

LaSalle School, 2001. *Photo by Carolyn Blackmon.*

confessionals until caught at it by a young priest and venomously chastised. This condition is now alleviated by the donation of the Fiedler heirs for a playground, the site on Eugenie between North Park Avenue and Orleans Street, where the Fiedler factory for making dress trimmings once stood.

On days when class-room windows were open, we heard the rattle of the shuttles of factory machinery from the east, the pounding of hammers in the Gold Leaf shop on Sedgwick Street (bordering the alley west of the school), and the tingling of the bells on the harness of the horses in use on the Sedgwick Street street cars whose barn adjoined the school yard on the north.

This is a good place to mention Ann Trimingham, the supervisor of drawing in the grammar schools, who, on her periodical visit to LaSalle School, would pass the empty lots now occupied by the Crilly Court Apartments [built in 1893]. When doing so, she would gather arms full of weeds growing wild all over these lots, which resembled the Acanthus Leaf, which grows equally wild in Greece and Sicily. These she would use for free-hand drawing instruction, as the folds of the leaves lend themselves to light and shade delineations.

From the sixth grade classroom, we could watch the extension of the square tower of St. Michael's Church, now topped with a steeple surmounted with a metal cross. Having seen this cross on the pavement of Eugenie Street extending from curb to curb line before hoisting into place, we could not visualize how small it now seems. The line of demarcation of the original brick tower and the extension can still be discerned by the difference of the brickwork in color and texture.

When his eighth graduation rolled around, Leo solicited an ad from Proudfoot's Bakery on Center Street (Armitage) for the program. Unfortunately, the printer used an "l" instead of a "t" when setting up the ad, so the final copy read "Proudfool's Bakery." Understandably (or not) Proudfoot refused to pay, and the graduating class went into the red for the program cost—not the best last memory of Leo's elementary school days.

And Back to Hudson

The Weissenborn family made one last move within the Old Town Triangle. In 1924, they settled into a three-story brick house at 1924 North Hudson, their home in the neighborhood. Having graduated from the LaSalle

School by then, Leo had enrolled at the old Chicago English High and Manual Training School in 1893. He wrote that "this school, located on Monroe Street near Halsted, was later replaced by the Crane and Lane High Schools or colleges." Actually, Mr. Weissenborn's memory was a little faulty. The English High and Manual Training School was founded as a males-only school at Twelfth Street and Michigan Avenue in 1890. Moving forward, in 1903, the school relocated to 2245 West Jackson Boulevard on Chicago's near west side. It was renamed in honor of businessman Richard T. Crane. Between 1911 and 1969, the school shared its building with Crane College, the first junior college in Chicago—hence the college connection in Leo's mind. The Crane College moved out in 1969 and is now known as Malcolm X College.

Other recollections of Weissenborn's high school years included the World's Columbian Exposition in 1893 and, for whatever reason, the family's "rosewood square piano, which was half an octave short. This piano was replaced with an upright." In the same sentence, he added, "We kids, with our savings, bought our first bookcase with glazed door to supplement our old walnut what-not." He noted also that his house was "flanked by wooden houses, many with front outside stairs leading to second floors, which are still prevalent around this neighborhood." Funny the things kids remember.

THE BUSINESS OF OLD TOWN IS BUSINESS

During the boom times of the late nineteenth century, Leo Weissenborn witnessed the growth of many businesses in Old Town. Piper's Bakery at 1610 North Wells Street was one of the largest and most important commercial establishments in the neighborhood. Piper's began as a mom and pop operation before the Great Fire (he baked the bread, and she sold it door-to-door). The original building burned to the ground in the fire, but Piper, like many other pioneering Old Towners, rebuilt on the same site, making the new bakery even bigger and more magnificent than the original—with an imposing façade and a magnificent Victorian interior. It became one of the busiest bakeries in the Midwest, employing more than five hundred people and shipping its products to thirty-nine states.

Next to the bakery was the Fick and Shute Private School, which, according to Leo, graduated a good many prominent citizens. One of these was Felix Riesenberg, a member of Walter Wellman's ill-fated expedition to the North

Pole. Riesenberg traveled with Wellman to Norway in an attempt to learn about ice conditions around the archipelago of Spitsbergen and to find a shortcut to the North Pole. They sailed for Spitsbergen on a Norwegian ice steamer, the *Ragnvald Jari*, and in early May pitched camp on the shores of Virgo Harbor, Danes Island. Later that month, they sailed north and east, landing at the Seven Islands. They were forced to leave the *Ragnvald Jari*, continuing on in sledges and aluminum board. They had not gone very far when a courier overtook them and reported that ice had forced the *Jari* to hole up along the western shore of Walden Island. Wellman sent part of his crew to rescue those stranded aboard the ship and proceeded north. But by this time, the summer sun had warmed the pack ice to slush and made travel very dangerous. With the sledges useless, the dogs were shot. Riesenberg and his crew mates had to haul their aluminum boats back to Walden Island, where they were rescued. He later gained fame as an author and wrote a bestseller called *East Side–West Side*.

Elsie Schumm Berwick, another illustrious graduate of Fick and Shute, became a physician and did her postgraduate medical work in Zurich, Switzerland. Her brother, also a graduate, attended West Point and became a colonel in the U.S. Army. He had the distinction of being buried in Arlington Cemetery next to Admiral Perry.

Around the corner, at 410 North Avenue, George and Emma Heller Schumm edited the *Alliance*, a weekly newspaper founded by the Reverend George C. Miln, a well-known Unitarian minister and Shakespearian lecturer. Mrs. Schumm was a women's rights advocate who lectured on the subject in the old Central Music Hall at State and Randolph Streets, later occupied by Marshall Field's Department Store and now Macy's. The Schumms moved to Boston, where George became a magazine editor. He ended his career on the staff of the *Nation* magazine in New York City.

Farther down on North Avenue was a thriving antique trunk store that catered to the needs of a population that could now afford to travel nationwide and worldwide. At 332 West North Avenue was another popular Old Town establishment, the Recher Wine and Liquor Company. This firm only stayed in the area for a few years, from 1907 to 1917. It later merged with the Pacific Wine Company.

Business was good in Old Town. Very good, indeed. During these glory days, before the advent of the aforementioned cable cars, sightseeing carriages picked up tourists at the Germania Club on Clark Street and drove them west though the business and residential districts of Old Town.

Newspapermen, writers, artists, lawyers and manufacturers came through. Some liked what they saw so much that they decided to buy property in the neighborhood and built two- and three-story houses. Old Town was also a transportation hub for Chicago. The North Chicago City Railway (NCRR) built huge stables on Orleans Street (where the current LaSalle School stands). At that time, the NCRR used fifteen hundred horses to draw its 250 cars. A repair shop for the carriages was constructed at Eugenie and North Park.

Manufacturing played a prominent part in Old Town's thriving business economy at the end of the nineteenth century. The first large factory to come in was the Deering Harvester Company, a manufacturer of farm equipment. William Deering was a dry goods wholesaler who had been doing business in Maine and New York. He built his first harvester in Plano, Illinois, southwest of the city. In 1880, he brought the factory to Chicago. At its height, the business employed over five thousand people. South of the horse car barns was a gold leaf factory owned by the Schwartz family. There, goldbeaters (remember Joseph O'Connell) flattened hunks of gold into sheets with copper-covered mallets. The Cheyney brothers bought looms and established a prosperous silk factory on the northwest corner of Eugenie and North Park Streets. Just east of LaSalle School was the Fiedler Silk and Wool Factory, built in 1914, to manufacture buttons and dress ornaments. Another large fabric company, just outside Old Town on Blackhawk Street, was Baum's Silk Mills.

Other manufacturing establishments in—or just out of—Old Town were the Western Wheel Works on Schiller, Oscar Mayer on Sedgwick and a soap factory on North Avenue between North Park and Sedgwick. A short distance away, there was an icehouse that sold to both domestic homes and commercial establishments. Heavier industries were located west of Halsted Street. Standing in the Newberry Schoolyard on any given day, one could hear two hundred factory whistles announcing the start, lunch break and end of a working day.

The streets of Leo Weissenborn's Old Town in 1890 look pretty much the same as the streets of Old Town today. Only their names were different. Armitage Avenue was Center Street. Lincoln Park West was North Park. North Park was Franklin. Orleans was Hammond. St. Paul was Florimond. Willow was Tell Court. And Concord was Starr Street. At the century's close, the last four streets had not been paved.

SOME INTERESTING NEIGHBORS AND ALMOST THE FIRST FAMILIES OF OLD TOWN

Leo had vivid remembrances of his Old Town neighbors, which reveal a lot about the ethnic and social diversity of the neighborhood. He wrote that

> *the six flat building at the corner of Hammond [Orleans] and Tell Court [Willow] had some interesting tenants. Gustave Harter headed the electrical construction company which put in the lowest bid for the electrical installations of the World's Columbian Exposition in 1892. However, he had little credit, so the wire manufacturers refused to furnish him with the wire necessary to do the job.*
>
> *When Charles Yerkes, the street railway baron, gave an electric fountain to Lincoln Park, he installed and operated same. Another interesting commission executed by Gustave Harter was to pull an electric cable across the Chicago River. The old LaSalle Street tunnel under the river had a three-inch diameter pipe along a sidewalk which was utilized in the following manner: a strong cord was tied to a rat's tail and let loose at one end of the pipe and released when it came out at the opposite end. The wire could then be started through by means of the cord.*
>
> *The John D. Kohlsaat family lived in a flat building at the corner of Sedgwick and Tell Court [Willow] Mr. Kohlsaat was a cousin of Judge Christian Kohlsaat and of H.H. Kohlsaat, who, when he became wealthy, bought and published the* Chicago Herald, *later the* Record Herald.

Leo Weissenborn judged the caliber of Old Town by the prestige of its families. Among his celebrated "First Citizens of Old Town" was George Schleifforth (1848–1921), a John Philip Sousa "wannabe" who composed fifty-six marches and other light popular tunes under his own name, as well as eleven others under the name of George Maywood. One of the most often hummed was "Every American Girl Is a Queen." An avid William Jennings Bryan supporter, Schleifforth wrote a march for his idol, "The William Jennings Bryan Democratic Success March."

Philip Henrici, another member of the Weissenborn elite, owned one of the oldest and finest restaurants in Chicago, the eponymous Henrici's, located on Randolph Street in the heart of the theater district. Weissenborn boasted that Henrici was an Old Town neighbor (the family lived on Wisconsin Street, near the Weissenborns' Hudson Street home). He was even prouder to claim that the Henrici children were his classmates, along with Ira Frank, who became a well-known physician, and the children of the saloon-owning Koenigsbergs.

Henrici was born in Austria and came to Chicago by way of New York. He opened his first lunch counter on State and Washington (site of Marshall Field's Department Store and later Macy's), where his Viennese pastries were the talk of the city. His Randolph Street restaurant opened in 1893, during the Columbian Exposition. He decorated the restaurant in the style of a Viennese coffeehouse, with stained-glass windows and a pastry counter in the window to attract passersby. It quickly became the "in" place to go for politicians and celebrities. The restaurant was torn down in 1962 to make way for the Civic Center (later renamed Daley Center—but Weissenborn had no way of knowing that).

Also on Weissenborn's list of notable Old Town residents were the Rendtorffs, who lived on the northeast corner of Lincoln Park West and Menomonee Streets. One son, Edmund, was a professor, who taught at the Lake Forest Academy for nearly twenty-five years. Another son, Walter, became a physician. He joined the U.S. Indian Service and became government physician at the Carlisle Indian School in Pennsylvania. Leo noted that during Walter's tenure there, the school's football team was world champion. The Rendtorffs' wealth and prominence came from their stove-board factory on Mohawk Street, near North Avenue. Stove boards were sheets of tile, wood, glass or other fire-resistant material used to frame the floor in front of a fireplace or surround a wood/coal stove—a necessary adjunct in the days of wood or coal-burning kitchen ranges.

Nor did individuals have to be prominent in their own right to make Leo's elite list. He noted that, during their tenure on Hudson Street, his mother became friendly with a neighbor living on Sedgwick Street—directly across the alley from their house. The neighbor's name was Mrs. Campbell, and she had the distinction of being the sister of the celebrated U.S. statesman Carl Schurz.

Another of the famous-by-association families were the Tevens. Mr. Teven was associated with Joseph Byfield, an immigrant from Hungary whose family owned an inn in a small town near Budapest. Joseph came to Chicago in 1867 and went to work in a State Street dry goods store owned by Marshall Field and Levi Z. Leiter. Joseph was said to be a "human calculator" in bookkeeping and soon moved up the ladder in the business, which ultimately became Marshall Field & Company. During the Great Fire of 1871, Joseph gained favor with his employers by helping move goods out of the path of the fire, which destroyed the store. Joseph and his brother decided to go into business on their own. They opened a cloak and suit manufacturing company where Teven worked. Byfield decided to go back into the family business and purchased the Sherman House at Clark and Randolph Streets.

Teven's daughter, Ella, married Aaron Jones, who had started his career as a candy salesman in the old Hooley's Theatre, later the Powers Theatre, on Randolph Street, which was taken over by Mr. Byfield's Sherman House. Jones became the head of Jones, Linick and Schaefer, builders and managers of Chicago's leading motion picture theaters.

An associate of Aaron Jones at Hooley's was Elmer Arminger, who worked as a cash boy (a messenger who carried money received by salesmen from a customer to a cashier and returned with the proper change) at Marshall Field's. Elmer lived with his widowed mother in a room on Center Street (Armitage). He ate dinner with the Weissenborns every evening and then took tray to his mother. The young man later took a job with a South Water Street produce merchant who sold egg crates and butter tubs as a sideline. At first, Elmer managed this business, but when it became so profitable, he decided to do it on his own. He started manufacturing the crates and tubs and was an instant success. During the First World War, he enhanced his prestige by being designated a buyer for the British government.

"This was early Chicago," writes Weissenborn,

> *at a time when the city was building its name and fame, rising Phoenix-like from ashes. My memories of those days are associated with Old Town. It wasn't called that then, of course. It's Old Town now because so many things remain to remind one of Chicago as it was the better part of a century ago.*

Old Town thanks you, Leo, for your memories.

10

EXTRAORDINARY PEOPLE

History is a kind of introduction to more interesting people than we can possibly meet in our restricted lives; let us not neglect the opportunity.
—Dexter Perkins

Through the years, Old Town has been home to some extraordinary people—many well known, others not so much. Until now, they have remained hidden in its illustrious past. Its time to bring them out and shine a light on them for all to see and appreciate.

Imagine a party in Old Town in the 1960s. Imagine that the most creative and interesting people living on what is arguably its most famous street, Crilly Court, were invited. Imagine that everybody came and that by some time-traveling legerdemain, you were there. Here are the people you would have met and the milieu in which you would have landed.

RICHARD LATHAM, 1920–1991: A DESIGNING MAN, A HIDDEN STORY

In this world of ordinary people, extraordinary people, I'm glad there is you.
—Jimmy Dorsey, 1947

Resting in the annals of Old Town's hidden history is a man whose talents and inventions are familiar to many of you but whose name probably is not.

That man is Richard Latham, one of the most brilliant industrial designers of all time and, as the saying goes, someone you should know.

What Do You Do For A Living

When Mande Latham was a little girl, her classmates asked her—as classmates do—" What does your father do for a living?"

Mande had no idea, so she went home and posed the question to her father. "You go back to your school tomorrow," he answered, "and tell your friends to walk around their houses. Have them look in the kitchen drawers, open the cabinets, check the shelves and pass by the refrigerator. I designed something in every one of them."

Indeed, he did. He ran the household design gamut: refrigerators, cabinetry and every conceivable utensil for the Eco Company, including spatulas, spoons, egg beaters and knives. It is a testament to his genius that Eco is still in business today and still producing items that Dick Latham designed.

Unlike Joseph O'Connell, Richard Latham was not self-taught. He was born in Kansas City, Missouri, in 1920 and studied engineering at the Kansas City Engineering School. He left Kansas City to study at the Armour Institute in Chicago, now the Illinois Institute of Technology (IIT). From 1940 to 1942, he was a protégé of the internationally renowned architect Mies van der Rohe. In 1942, he worked briefly as a designer for Montgomery Ward and then went on to serve his country in World War II. In 1945, following his military service, he joined the Raymond Loewy Design Firm in Chicago.

Dick Latham was a most amazing talent. He worked on the design of the Greyhound Bus Scenicruiser, a two-level bus, in collaboration with General Motors. He created interior spaces for airplanes. He designed Hallicrafters' SX radio receiver in 1945. In 1952, he worked on Borg Erickson's Model 1500 "Flight" bathroom scale, selected by *Fortune* magazine as one of the top five hundred designs of all time. He was responsible for the red, white and blue logo for the old Standard Oil Company and for the smokestack of the *Queen Mary* luxury ocean liner. In recognition of all his achievements, he was made director of design at Lowey's Chicago office.

Latham spent five years working with the Rosenthal Company, a well-known German porcelain manufacturer. He was the prime mover behind the design of Rosenthal's 1952 Studio Line. Dick had influenced Philip Rosenthal, head of the firm that had been founded by his father in 1879, to establish a separate division to produce the Studio Line. That line won a Grand Prize at the Brussels World Fair in 1958 and was later shown in special venues known as "Studio Houses" worldwide. Over the next thirty years, Studio Line employed more than one hundred designers from eleven nations. Dick's dinnerware, designed for the Studio Line, is in the permanent collection of the Museum of Modern Art in New York.

In 1955, Dick left Lowey to found his own design firm, Latham Tyler Jensen, Inc. He was joined by two other Lowey designers: Robert D. Tyler and George Jensen. The accolades kept coming. He was made president of the American Society of Interior Design (ASID) in 1959 and president of the International Council of Societies of Industrial Design (ICSID) in 1965. He was advocate of international design opportunities and cooperation. In 1970, he became a pioneer in the new area of industrial design and founded another company, Richard S. Latham & Associates, Inc., which specialized in product planning. He also acted as design advisor for Bang and Olufsen, a Danish firm that designed and manufactured audio products, television sets and telephones. In the midst of all this, he found time to co-found Land's End, which enjoyed immediate success and is still going strong today. Extraordinary!

The Man, His House and His Music

Dick and Mary Ann Latham found their way to 1706 Crilly Court, former home of the O'Tooles, in the 1950s. It's curious how many creative people discovered Crilly Court and how their lives came together. In 1954, the Lathams applied for a loan to buy the Crilly property, but their bank turned them down saying that they would be wasting their money because the neighborhood was a ghetto. In fact, although Crilly Court had experienced a renaissance after a number of young urban pioneers moved in, the Old Town neighborhood, especially west of North Park Avenue around St. Michael's Church, had become infested with gangs and gypsies and had a bad reputation. But Mary Ann and Dick had faith in the spirit of the neighborhood and the potential for urban renewal. They were so angry with the bank, given their financial status and good credit rating, that they withdrew their money from that institution and walked across the street to a rival bank, which happily accepted their account and gave them a house loan. Officers of this bank, no doubt, recognized that Old Town was on the verge of economic and social growth and that it had become home to a diverse and stable population: young married couples, artists, journalists, designers, media people and other professionals. The Lathams fit right in.

This Old House

In 1964, Dick Latham undertook a revolutionary rehab of the property at 1706 North Crilly Court—what else would you expect from a revolutionary designer? In a bold move, he gutted the house, top to bottom. Gone were the small rooms. Gone was the traditional main-floor living room, dining room, parlor and kitchen configuration. Gone were the front porch and second-floor entry stairs. (He could never have done this today. The neighborhood received landmark status in 1978, making it impossible to change the façades of the old houses.) He moved the family living space to the lower level and placed the kitchen, master bedroom and laundry area there. Mary Ann bolted a circular top on an old Eames table and made this a creative center where they designed boats (both were avid sailors), built models and came up with new design products. Richard designed the products and wrote articles about them; Mary Ann acted as editor in chief and project supervisor.

The main floor of the house was transformed into a music theater with state-of-the-art stereo equipment, floor-to-ceiling speakers and near-perfect acoustics. It was open front to back. With that, the Lathams brought music to Crilly Court—just as Joseph O'Connell brought it to Eugenie Street, except that O'Connell played his violin and Latham manipulated his stereo.

People came from all over the world to listen to music at the Lathams'. Jazz musicians dropped in after their gigs to jam. Music critics came to let their hair down and listen. Friends popped by to party and enjoy. On many occasions, the festivities got so loud that some neighbors would call to complain. Of course, no one answered the phone because it was impossible to hear over the music, so the police were summoned. The doorbell would ring, and an officer would issue a warning. More often than not, the Lathams invited the officer in, and the party continued with the blessing of Chicago's finest. Neighbors who couldn't go with the beat moved away.

So Long, Farewell

So, good-bye dear and Amen,
Here's hoping we meet now and then,
It was great fun,
But it was just one of those things.
—Cole Porter

Mary Ann and Dick Latham had a wonderful life together. Summer days were spent sailing. Winter nights were spent listening to the music of their era: Tommy Dorsey, Count Basie, Frank Sinatra, Duke Ellington, Glen Miller and Glen Gould, all played at full volume. Mary Ann and Dick were probably the only parents in the neighborhood who played music louder than their children, and the kids loved to hang out there. They were an ideal couple. Dick always said that Mary Ann made him who he was. Maybe he was right. She proofread everything he ever wrote, studied his designs, made corrections and gave him the go-ahead when a project was okay. A perfect pair.

Latham changed American life with his designs. He also gave back to the society that accepted his work with such enthusiasm. He endowed a foundation at IIT to help young designers get ahead in the world. With all his acclaim and achievement, Dick remained a very practical, unassuming and down-to-earth man. When asked about his theory of design, he replied, "Chicago is a horse collar town. Design is there to pull the wagon—not decorate the horse."

Richard Latham died in 1991; Mary Ann died ten years later. Crilly Court is a less colorful place without them. But if, on some warm summer night, you happen to be walking past the house at 1706 and you hear laughter behind the ghostly melody emanating from Tommy Dorsey's trombone, don't be alarmed. It's just those music-loving Lathams having another great party.

OH RARE HENRY RAGO:
AN EXTRAORDINARY POET 1915–1969

Had I the heavens' embroidered cloths enwrought with golden and silver light,
The blue and the dim and the dark cloths of night and light and the half light,
I would spread the cloths under your feet:
But I, being poor, have only my dreams; I have spread my dreams under
your feet;
Tread softly, because you tread on my dreams.
—William Butler Yeats

Henry Rago was a Renaissance man, a poet's poet who edited *Poetry* magazine for fourteen years, from 1955 to 1969—the longest editorship of anyone since Harriet Monroe. He was a professor of literature at the University of Chicago, having joint tenure with the Divinity School and the new Collegiate Division, where he co-chaired the program in history and the philosophy of religion. His seminars and research were interdisciplinary studies of the relationship between poetry and religion. During his short and productive life, Rago's poems were widely published in magazines and newspapers, beginning at age sixteen in *Poetry* magazine. His book of poems, *A Sky of Late Summer*, was published in 1963. He was an always-available mentor who guided young poets and essayists through their productive and often trying years, admonishing them about drug and alcohol use and advising them on how to make public presentations. The phone would ring late at night, and it might be any one of the people whose volumes you will find in the poetry section of bookstores and libraries today. Sometimes, the messages his young daughter took were straightforward. Other times, they were downright bizarre, as was the case in the following conversation:

Caller: "Yeah, this is _____. Tell him the, uh, tell him the owl is white and has, uh, um, glowing eyes."

Rago's daughter: "All right, I'm writing this down, 'the owl is white'…"

Caller: "Yeah, and the eyes…well, he'll know what I'm talking about."

(More information followed.)

Rago's aughter: "Yes, yes I understand. I will give this to him first thing in the morning."

Caller: "Read this back to me."

And she read it back. When the caller was satisfied, the note was left on her father's pillow so he would find it when he awoke.

Famed poet Gwendolyn Brooks once said that she owed Henry Rago her life. "I'm so lucky. Henry was so good to me. I loved your father."

Henry Rago was held in high regard among his peers. One contemporary, Stanley Kunitz, wrote, "The best of his poems, of which 'The Knowledge of Light' is representative, reach an astonishing depth of simplicity. They achieve a kind of claritas, the splendor of the true."

Another contemporary, Hayden Carruth, commented on his book:

> *These are rare and beautiful poems by an exceedingly rare poet. I mean that Henry Rago, who began with a surpassing lyrical talent and a mind as quick as a fish, has stood off the blandishments of his own abilities; which is a more particular way of saying that he has resisted the temptations of poetry. His poems are natural, sure, and right; without one surrender to the siren of virtuosity. Hence they have a grace and purity, which come only from true things, and a trueness, which comes only to tempered things. In*

these splendid, almost unbelievable poems, Rago brings back the crystalline, Arielesque quality that poets forty years ago considered indispensable— compression with density; harmony without artifice. I find these poems continually rewarding.

Rago recorded his poems for the Library of Congress and for the Lamont Library at Harvard. He traveled worldwide, lecturing on literature and philosophy and reading his poetry—all of which tells us something about the poet and the professor. But to really understand the man and his work, we must take him back to the place where he lived, received much of his inspiration and shared his enormous gifts with people he loved and respected—to Old Town and to Crilly Court.

The Fabulous Sixties

Henry Rago moved to Crilly Court in 1962 with his wife, Juliet, and his children, Maria Christina (ten), Maria Carmela (nine), Anthony Pascal (seven) and Maria Martha (four). They took their place among the other creative and creating people who gathered in Old Town in the '60s— Richard and Mary Ann Latham, Herman and Marilew Kogan, Harry and Kitty Weese, Paul and Vesta Angle, Jon and Jennifer Anderson, Slim and Gladys Williams and Hoke Norris, among others.

It was an exciting time for people of talent and vision in and out of Old Town, a time when they could mingle and exchange ideas with others who were young and gifted and changing the nation's cultural landscape: Woodstock ushered in the psychedelic '60s. Peter, Paul and Mary were asking "Where Have All the Flowers Gone?" and leading a folk music revival. The Beatles and Motown were turning the music world upside down. In politics, John F. Kennedy proved that a Roman Catholic could be elected president of the United States. Betty Friedan wrote *The Feminine Mystique*, effectively creating the modern women's movement. Dr. Martin Luther King led freedom marches and advocated nonviolent resistance to racism. Anti–Vietnam War groups organized and held public draft card burnings. And on June 27, 1969, at the Stonewall Inn, a hangout for gays on Christopher Street in New York, patrons physically resisted one of what had become a series of routine, anti-gay police raids, setting off a barrage of protests in the following days and marking a significant social shift at a time when few people were willing to be publicly identified as homosexual. New York City officials cited the event as the beginning of the gay rights movement—but Chicago officials proved otherwise by bringing to light the activities of Henry Gerber. Henry Gerber had established the Society for Human Rights on Crilly Court in Chicago in 1924, twenty-five years before Stonewall. The society was granted a charter by the State of Illinois in which its members' right to congregate and speak freely was affirmed.

The 1960s also saw a technological revolution with the dawning of the space age, culminating on July 21, 1969, at 4:17 p.m., when Neil Armstrong and Col Edwin Aldrin Jr. brought their ship to rest on a level, rock-strewn plain near the southwestern shore of the Sea of Tranquility on the moon. Armstrong radioed to Earth and mission control in Houston, Texas. "Houston, Tranquility Base here. The Eagle has landed." About six and a half hours later, Neil Armstrong opened the landing craft's hatch, stepped slowly down the ladder and declared, as he planted the first human footprint on the lunar surface, "That's one small step for man and one giant leap for mankind." Veteran newsman Walter Cronkite, watching and reporting, shook his head, laughed and exclaimed, "Whew Boy!" Whew Boy, indeed! Bliss it was in that dawn to be alive. But to be young was very much heaven.

This was the backdrop against which the extraordinary people of Crilly Court—Henry Rago, Richard Latham, Herman Kogan and Kitty Weese— lived and worked. The offspring of these incredibles—Mande Latham, Rick Kogan and the Rago siblings—documented their growing-up years in the 1960s Old Town and endowed us with a real sense of home and neighborhood life. The following narrative is based on the memoirs of Carmela Rago, Christina Rago Brown, Martha Rago, Anthony Rago and their mother, Juliet Rago.

Who Was Henry Rago—What Was He?

Henry Rago was a professor at the university during the chancellorship of acclaimed educational philosopher Robert Maynard Hutchins, renowned for eliminating varsity football at the university and creating the College of the University, which evolved into a pedagogical system built on the Great Books. He was also editor of *Poetry* magazine, whose offices were on Oak Street, a short walk from Old Town.

The Rago family moved to Crilly Court in 1962 from Chicago's south side. It was a life-changing move for the family, who had resided for many years in a small apartment "on the wrong side of" the University of Chicago's

Midway. The move to Old Town was the result of more than the availability of an apartment. On his many walks around Crilly Court, Henry Rago had become enchanted with the neighborhood. It was a far cry from the Hyde Park neighborhood. The sidewalks were clean. There was no garbage, loose papers or dirt flying around. Houses were kept up, window and doorframes were freshly painted. Pink and white blossoming dogwood trees lined the parkway. Crilly porches overflowed with petunias and fascinating people. It was exactly the kind of place where Henry Rago wanted to live and raise his children.

Henry first took the family to what would become their Old Town home, the first-floor apartment at 1707 North Park overlooking Crilly Court, in the spring of 1962. It was empty then so that they could take in its spaciousness. There were three bedrooms to accommodate the family of six, which was heaven after the cramped space to which they had become accustomed. The pine floors had just been stripped and sanded and glistened like honey. The walls were painted white, and there was an old working fireplace in the living room. Outside the living room windows, the dogwoods were in bloom.

On a second visit—with their arrival imminent—Henry took the children to Crate and Barrel on Wells Street and allowed each one to pick out a colorful tin mug, which would be for his or her exclusive use. They also selected matching towels, a mark of their father's strong sense of precision and army-style order. (Carmela's was navy blue.) Still another visit led to Mr. Dawg—a hot dog stand at the end of the Old Town Triangle on Lincoln Park West and the ghost of Ogden Avenue. The elder Rago had a weakness for hand-cut French fries and simple comfort foods: hot dogs, hamburgers and Italian beef sandwiches with the works. The trips to Mr. Dawg became a ritual before and after the family moved in

When the children lived in Hyde Park, they attended the very strict St. Thomas the Apostle Catholic School. The move north allowed them to enroll at more progressive institutions: the LaSalle Elementary School and Francis W. Parker High School. They could walk to their respective schools—down the block from their North Park home to LaSalle, and through beautiful Lincoln Park to Francis Parker. Their father could walk to his Oak Street office—taking a different route each time, depending on the weather and time of year. It was on these walks that he composed letters he wanted to write to fellow poets about their work and to come up with ideas for new poems. Once back at Crilly, he would gather the family round and share interesting aspects of his day at the *Poetry* offices.

Once in Love With Crilly

Crilly Court was the place to be in the 1960s—both for its physical features and for the denizens of the literary world who gathered there. Juliet Rago, the family matriarch, found the community unique in a big city like Chicago—a microcosm, actually. There were newspaper people like Hoke Norris, Herman Kogan and Jon Anderson; television people like Dave Garroway and Don Herbert (Mr. Wizard); adventurers like Slim Williams; and an assortment of artists, musicians, businesspeople, hair dressers and shopkeepers all living in the various apartments, stacked up four stories. Picture a series of brick buildings whose wrought-iron back porches formed four tiers in the courtyard where neighbors congregated: "We would meet each other constantly," Juliet recalled,

> *going to work, going to the grocery store, with or without kids, just strolling, chatting, or announcing some important news. Sometimes, there might even*

Crilly Courtyard, the home and playground of some of the 1960s' most creative people. *Photo by Norman Baugher.*

be an argument over the back fence. Most of the time, however, people were quite civil and friendly and could be counted on for help of any kind. Everyone knew everyone else and kept an eye on all the children. We had a rule that none of them was to leave the Court. If any did, parents went scouting about the streets to find them. One day, Martha decided to wander over to LaSalle School, about a block west of us, to try the swings in the playground. We searched frantically for her until Hoke Norris triumphantly came around the corner into the courtyard with Martha in his arms. That was our community.

Inside-Outside, All Around the Court

The Rago porch, on the first floor of one of the buildings, was flanked by a flower bed that ran along the porch and was filled with red, white and pink annuals. In warm weather, Juliet, a gifted artist, would set up her easel on the porch to paint while the kids were in school. When they came home in the afternoon, they would hang onto the railing to watch what she was doing. Juliet sometimes held impromptu drawing classes for them—the genesis of the renowned Crilly Court Art Fair organized by the Kogan boys.

Henry and Juliet Rago entertained their literary friends on the deck in the late spring, summer and fall. In the winter, the family retired to the living room, which had been cordoned off from the rest of the boxcar-like apartment to give it a more elegant, drawing room feel. The space was furnished in Danish modern décor. There was a dining table, leather-seated chairs, a sleek sofa and a piano—all positioned around the fireplace. Although the apartment was small, it never seemed cramped because of the arrangement of furniture, the design aesthetic and the tasteful balance of color and size.

Every gathering was a "happening," where Henry held court and Juliet sang and played the piano or guitar. Sometimes the guest list consisted exclusively of poets. Among these was James Dickey, one of the nation's most distinguished modern poets, as well as a critic, lecturer, teacher, musician and novelist, probably best known for his dark novel *Deliverance*, later adapted into a critically acclaimed movie. Dickey would play Juliet's guitar—once even giving her a pick to keep. Donald Hall, poet laureate of the United States and consultant in poetry to the Library of Congress, could be found among the guests with his wife, Jane Kenyon, also a poet and honored as poet laureate of New Hampshire. Other times, there was a mix of artists, poets, musicians and university people—like Mircea Eliade, a

Romanian historian of religion, fiction writer, philosopher and professor at the University of Chicago; James Redfield, the Edward Olson Distinguished Service Professor, also at the University of Chicago; and novelist Saul Bellow, whose Chicago stories won him two Pulitzer Prizes, three National Book Awards and a Nobel Prize for Literature. Neighborhood musicians came to talk, listen and entertain, sustained by Juliet's famed buffet dinners—chicken in aspic or veal scaloppini, a green salad, crusty bread, Italian pastries and an unending supply of coffee and wine. All the guests were interesting and different. The Ragos lived among and gathered together bohemians, artists, writers, psychologists, architects, filmmakers and performers who had in common an appreciation of art and people.

Christina and Carmela would lie in bed and listen to the music, the laughter and the conversation. When the guests left, they would sneak into the living room and sample what was left in the brandy glasses. Christina recalled a night when the eminent American poet Robert Frost was there and invited her to sit on his knee. Afterward, her father joked, "Now you can tell your grandchildren that you sat on Robert Frost's knee."

Meet the Neighbors

The North Park apartment complex and the Crilly row houses constituted a kind of cultural Chicago who's who. Filmmaker Chuck Olin, who lived across the courtyard from the North Park complex, gave Christina her first job with the Film Group of Chicago. He rode a bright red motorcycle and parked it at the end of the courtyard. (If someone tried that today, it would be gone in five minutes.) Popular model Jennifer Anderson and her husband, newspaperman Jon Anderson, added their cachet to the entourage from an apartment above the Ragos. Jennifer had a weekly beauty column in the *Chicago Tribune*; Jon was a regular *Tribune* columnist. Newspaperwoman Virginia Kay also lived on one of the upper floors with her two daughters, both of whom befriended Christina. Lisa, the younger daughter, became a writer. Suzie, the elder daughter, chose psychology as her profession. Another neighbor, Lois Axeman was a freelance illustrator for *Highlights* magazine and worked from her home studio. The girls came to watch her work and admire the tools of her craft: paints, inks and markers. Lois illustrated Jennifer Anderson's publication, *The Thinking Woman's Beauty Book*. James Axeman was a collage artist and graphic designer. He held a much-anticipated annual holiday party where neighbors gathered to make

Christmas decorations: tissue paper snowflakes one year and baked clay ornaments the next (which everyone had a hand in painting once they were dry). Like most other Crilly residents, the Axemans were music lovers. Jim's jazz-themed parties were legendary among neighbors.

Slim Williams and his wife lived two buildings over from the Ragos. Born in 1881, Slim was an arctic explorer who came to Chicago on a dog sled for the World's Fair in 1933. Martha Rago suspected he was trying to call attention to the need for highway development in Alaska. He was successful. But publicizing Alaska's need for highways was not Slim's only Chicago accomplishment. He was also a fabulous storyteller. With his second wife, Gladys, they settled among other members of the city's avant-garde in the North Park apartments. He was an affable man, with a friendly face and open grin. He used a cane to get around, although he was tall and erect. From his rocking chair on the back deck, he played out the Crilly version of *Rear Window*, keeping watch over the goings-on in the courtyard below. He would invite the children, individually and collectively, up for lemonade and regale them with stories about Eskimos, life in the Arctic and life on the court. He wrote two children's books about his North Pole adventures: the first, *Friend of the Singing One*, in 1967 and the second, *The Long Hungry Night*, in 1973, just a year before his death at age ninety-two.

Kids' Life

Martha, Carmela, Christina and Anthony lived in a world of kids—kids who played together, kids who babysat, kids who explored and kids who just hung out. Juliet said that they had only been in the apartment a few days when she opened the back door and found a little red-haired girl sitting on the porch. Asked who she was and what she was doing there, the child announced that she was waiting for Carmela to wake up so she could play with her. Her name, she announced with authority, was Annie Russinof. The Russinofs, it turned out, lived across the courtyard in one of the Crilly row houses. Her father, Roy, had a popcorn wagon and fudge stand on Wells Street south of North Avenue; her mother, Pat, was a nurse.

In the first week of their Crilly residence, Carmela made friends with Katie Rutherford. On Carmela's initial visit to the Rutherford house, Katie's mother pulled out the *Chicago Social Register* and, after pouring herself a martini, said, "Let me see if you are in here." She leafed through the Rs. "Oh, you're not," she said.

Carmela grabbed the book herself and searched for "Rago." It was not there. So she went home and related the experience to her father. "You tell her I'm in *Who's Who of American Poets*," he snarled. The next day, Carmela rang the Rutherford's bell and announced, "My father said to tell you that he's in *Who's Who of American Poets*, have you heard of it?" There was a dramatic pause.

"Oh my dear, yes I have," Mrs. Rutherford answered. "They probably just left your names out of the *Social Register* by accident."

Anthony was quickly inducted into the Crilly kids' world. He was invited to the Kogans' house. As a "welcome to the Crilly courtyard, they gave him one of their treasured possessions: a Curious George collection. Anthony reciprocated by mercilessly tormenting Rick Kogan and his friends: stealing their game equipment, shouting taunts and throwing dirt clods. Rick, however, was not to be picked on—especially not by a younger kid. He fought back, giving as good or better than he got. Not knowing that his own child was the instigator, Henry Rago confronted the older boys and told them that he had been a boxer in the army and that he would happily take any of them on if they didn't leave his son alone. Unfazed, Rick laughed at him and made a smart remark. Rago managed to hold his temper—after all, young Kogan was only a boy—but he told Anthony in no uncertain terms to stay away from the bullies. As a parting shot, he said to Rick, "You made Mrs. Rago cry!" That did faze the ten-year-old.

Despite a rocky beginning, the Crilly kids became a close-knit group, pairing off by age, more or less, but joining forces for complex games—secret agent, kick the can and storytelling. They would sit on an old green bench in the courtyard at dusk and scare the bejesus out of one another with ghost stories until their parents called them to bed. The boys played baseball in the long courtyard, and the girls played tag and badminton. They all hung out over the basement steps and talked for hours. They even held their own Crilly Court Art Fair, the brainchild of the aforementioned ten-year old Rick Kogan—their pride and joy for the few years it was held. The entrepreneurial Kogan boys hung the art on the fence and negotiated the prices from ten cents to fifty cents.

When they weren't finding things to do in the courtyard, the Crilly kids went exploring. There were plenty of places to explore just around the Crilly corner: the streets of Old Town, the LaSalle Schoolyard and the Menomonee Club. Most of the Old Town and Crilly kids congregated at the Menomonee Club for special activities. Basil Kane got the boys into soccer, and Tony Matesi (a retired circus clown) taught tumbling. The

This page: Old Town kids. *Photos by Norman Baugher.*

tumbling team performed at the Old Town Art Fair and was even invited to appear on the old *Bozo's Circus* television show on WGN. The Menomonee Club also offered cooking classes, slot car races, Friday night movies with popcorn, Halloween costume parties, holiday festivals and even a Mr. and Miss Menomonee contest.

It was great being a '60s Old Town kid. Christina later said that as children, growing up in Crilly Court, they were under the illusion that they ruled the neighborhood. They probably did.

Fathers, and Sons and Daughters

Henry Rago was a devoted father. He took his children to concerts, plays, art exhibits and poetry readings. He instilled in them a love for both serious drama and comedy. They went to every Marx Brothers' festival the city held. Anthony even memorized many Harpo routines and performed them for his sisters.

Though he loved all his children dearly, Anthony was his father's special buddy—friend, foil, little soldier and comic soul mate. They would walk together, hand in hand, through the neighborhood—Henry Rago in his Brooks Brothers suit, Anthony in shorts with a jacket and tie, emulating a young Prince Charles. Often the boy would carry along a toy gun, an airplane or some Match Box cars purchased by his father.

Henry gave his son some wonderful books: *A Wrinkle in Time* by Madeline L'Engle, *Wind, Sand, and Stars* by Antoine de Saint Exupery, volumes of poetry, encyclopedias, histories and, just for fun, Hardy Boys mysteries. He also gifted him with model trains and cars, armies of tin soldiers from wars of all eras, building blocks, architecture kits and a guinea pig named Frisky. Anthony also had coin and stamp collections enriched with items from his father's worldwide travels and gifts from friends abroad.

Anthony learned to play chess, and he learned war games, chase and capture, negotiation and release of prisoners and Morse code. Henry Rago had served in the Office of Strategic Services throughout World War II. He was in London during the blitz and in Paris after the liberation. He brought back stories about blackouts, document destruction, code breaking and all sorts of information to set a child's imagination soaring. He did not share information about the horrors of war and the effect they had on his psyche for the rest of his life.

In the evening, Henry Rago listened to Anthony's prayers: "Our Father," "Hail Mary" and his recurrent plea that God help him refrain from his compulsion to climb porches. The girls would laugh at this request because they knew that the next day, there would be a call from a neighbor complaining, "He's out there again, three flights up." Carmela became her brother's keeper. If she saw him run out and start up, she would call to her mother, "Anthony's climbing the porches."

Between father and son there was a "signal" sound. After Anthony was in bed, Henry would wait about ten minutes and then he would knock on the wall. The boy would knock back, and his father would knock again. The signaling would go on until Anthony fell asleep.

The entire Rago family engaged in games and activities together, but only those that developed mental acuity and encouraged intellectual inquiry. One Christmas, a relative gifted them with games the elder Rago considered junk, so he bundled the offensive items up for regifting to less fortunate families in the neighborhood, for whom any games were a welcome present. Sharing and helping others was one of the important lessons Henry Rago passed on to his children.

A Life Well Lived

Like the Lathams, the Ragos were a perfect couple: talented, compatible and absolutely devoted to each other. They never called each other by first names—it was always "dear." They went everyplace together—to the Old Town School to hear folk music, to the Shrimp Boat to dance the "wooly bully" and to Twin Anchors for a burger and a beer. The neighbors loved them, and the children loved them. It was great fun for everyone to hang out at the Ragos'.

Henry Rago was a deeply religious man. Once they were established in the court, he joined St. Michael's Church. Before vacations, he established a practice of taking the family to St. Michael's for a "little visit." Even if the destination was only a couple hours from Chicago, they had to light candles to ensure their safe passage. He would lead them down the aisle and give each child a candle to light. Then they would kneel at the altar and say a prayer. Before leaving, they had to acknowledge the statues of every saint in the church.

Henry Rago loved music—all sorts of music: The Beatles, Miles Davis, Odetta, Harry Belafonte, Frank Sinatra. He particularly liked Harry Nillson's sentimental "Everybody's Talking," which his sixteen-year-old daughter found a little "cloying." But Henry treated the lyrics as though he had personally edited them and placed them in the *Poetry* magazine.

He could also be a jokester. He would walk down the streets of the Triangle—Eugenie, St. Paul or North Park—shouting, "Okay, everybody out for volley ball!" Neighbors just didn't know what to make of him.

Good-bye, Old Friend

Henry Rago died of a massive heart attack on May 26, 1969. He was only fifty-three years old. As they had during his life, neighbors gathered in the small kitchen to help out any way they could: preparing food, starting a phone tree, sweeping up, talking, keeping the family occupied with living. That's how it was on the court.

Rago's sudden death ended plans to travel in Europe, lecture and write. He had resigned his post with *Poetry* magazine, leaving as his legacy the largest subscription list in the magazine's history and enough money in the treasury to ensure its continued publication. In his years there, Rago had never missed a month of publication—although there were many times he had to reassure anxious printers that their money would be forthcoming. He was looking forward to meeting with poets abroad, sharing ideas and creating new works. Sadly, that did not happen.

Envoi

Only a moment: a moment of strength, of romance, of glamour, of youth!...A flick of sunshine upon a strange shore, the time to remember, the time for a sigh, and—goodbye.
—*Joseph Conrad*

Ah, how the distances spiral from that secrecy:
Room, rooms, roof spun to the huge midnight, and into
The rings and rings of stars.
—*Henry Rago*

Juliet Rago called the ten years the family lived in Crilly Court "the happiest time: a celebration of art and life that was palpable and contagious."

Martha recalled:

There were so many people I remember from Crilly Court who were interesting, not only because of their prominence on the Chicago art and intellectual scene, but because they and/or their children were part of a rich, dynamic and varied everyday life that was "the Court." It wasn't until I was an adult that I realized what an extraordinary thing it was to have such texture and richness all around me.

We will leave the Ragos' Crilly Court with Christina's benediction: "Perhaps, in our youth, we took too much for granted. I think I have spent my adulthood looking for a similar feeling of community in the places I have lived and never found such a place again."

KITTY BALDWIN WEESE: ALL THE THINGS SHE WAS

*You are the promised kiss of springtime that makes the lonely winter seem long,
You are the breathless hush of evening that trembles on the brink of a lovely song.
—Oscar Hammerstein and Jerome Kern*

Kitty Weese no longer stands behind the movable counter in her unique kitchen—designed by her husband, the distinguished architect Harry Weese—pouring wine or making cucumber sandwiches for friends. She does not climb the narrow stairs to her aerie on the fourth floor to create incomparable watercolor botanicals. And she does not point with pride to the artifacts that fill her house, explaining the provenance of each to first-time visitors. Kitty has left that building and walked into Old Town's hidden history.

The Story of Kitty

She spread the white painting surface on the table before her. She assembled the various colors she planned to use in its transformation. She arranged the items intended as the subjects of her painting and took the brush between her long, graceful fingers. She held it poised above the paper, waiting for the moment of creativity. Then, it came.

Kitty Weese was a southern lady, born and raised in Montgomery, Alabama. She embodied all the attributes of southern gentility: tall, willowy, soft-spoken, reserved, graceful and resolute, a true steel magnolia. She was kind, intelligent, talented and beautiful.

Those who knew Kitty associate her with the watercolor paintings that are her legacy. But her interests did not always lie in the area of art. She was a southern belle, but not a typical one. Throughout her life, she had a series of careers and succeeded in all of them. Along the way, she improved conditions within her chosen fields and made life better for those she touched.

She began as a child psychologist, studying first at the University of London and later at Huntingdon College in Alabama. She practiced both at the Children's Clinic in Richmond, Virginia, and in her home city of Montgomery, Alabama. When World War II broke out, she volunteered as a "Grey Lady" at the hospital in Montgomery, caring for boys in training to be pilots. Because of her background in psychology, the State Department hired her to find out what the young trainees were really thinking and to prepare them for the experience of war.

Her interest in the arts began during the war years, encouraged by her brother, the architect and interior designer Ben Baldwin. Ben graduated from Princeton in 1935 and had gone on to study painting with Hans Hofmann in Provincetown, Massachusetts, and New York, where he mingled with people prominent in the art world. In 1938, he went the Cranbrook Academy of Art in Detroit, Michigan, where he met a young Chicago architect named Harry Weese and briefly shared a practice with him. He introduced Kitty to Harry and, in Kitty's words, arranged the marriage, although that didn't happen for a while.

Ben joined the navy during World War II and was stationed both in New York and Washington, D.C., where he held a weekly salon for some of the country's leading painters, architects and designers. Kitty managed to get away from her hospital duties in Richmond on weekends to act as his hostess. She often said she was lucky to get her art and modern design education from the people who were actually shaping it. Her life was taking a fateful turn. At these gatherings, she reconnected with Harry Weese, although they had been carrying on a kind of correspondence courtship since their first meeting. In February 1945, just before he left for the Pacific, Harry and Kitty were married in the chaplain's office on the Brooklyn Bridge. It was to become a lifelong partnership.

Kitty and Harry

After the war, Harry and Kitty moved to Chicago. They were faced with the same problems as other returning veterans: housing shortages, small apartments when they could find them, growing families and limited budgets. What they really wanted and needed was affordable housing and well-designed home furnishings. The young Weeses believed that good design was essential, not just for the wealthy, but also for everyone who wanted to spend their lives surrounded by beautiful things.

During their first year in Chicago, Kitty jokingly said that she and Harry moved every five days. Mostly, they lived in hotels where one could only rent a room for five days without being considered a resident, which neither of them wanted. When they saw a sign in the window of an apartment building on Walton Street, just across the street from the Newberry Library, advertising a room for rent, they grabbed it. It was literally just a room with no private bath, but at least it was not a residence hotel.

Harry had spent a great deal of time in Europe in the 1930s. He was drawn to the design work of the Scandinavians and the way they blended woodworking with modern design. He became a protégé of the noted Finnish architect and designer Alvar Aalto. Aalto had a combination store, gallery and factory in Helsinki, where he displayed his own art and furniture creations, as well as those of other designers. This combined operation had such a profound influence on Harry that he decided he would one day start a similar enterprise in Chicago. It took him ten years to make that happen.

Kitty and Jody—Baldwin/Kingrey

Once they had settled in Chicago, Harry and Kitty found themselves in the company of a lively group of artists, architects and designers. On a Sunday afternoon in 1947, they were attending a party in Hyde Park and met a young woman named Jody Kingrey, who, as luck would have it, was looking for an outlet for her own creative energies. During the cocktail party conversation, an established interior designer in the group happened to remark what a shame it was that young veterans and their families had no place to buy good, affordable home furnishings. That was Harry's "aha" moment. He knew Alvar Aalto was visiting at Cranbrook, so he boarded a train to Detroit. With a handshake, he secured the Midwest franchise for Artek furniture (Aalto's line). On the way home from the train station, he saw a For Rent sign in a storefront on Ohio and Michigan. It was in the elegant art deco Holabird and Root Michigan Square Building. Just like that, he walked in and signed the lease. Impulsive, yes—but that was Harry.

Kitty, Harry and Jody were now in the home furnishing business. They called their enterprise Baldwin Kingrey. They each borrowed $3,000 from their parents and ordered $9,000 worth of furniture. Within three months, they were in the black. The store introduced Aalto's classic bentwood furniture design to Chicago and helped bring about the Scandinavian design boom of the 1950s. Aalto enthusiastically endorsed Baldwin Kingrey and started the trio on their road to success. Harry ran his architectural practice out of the back room of the store. And so, a series of seemingly unconnected events started a design revolution: some wartime "art get-togethers" in Washington; a chance remark at a cocktail party in Hyde Park; a handshake in Detroit; and a For Rent sign in a window on Michigan Avenue. History. That same year, Kitty made more history; she opened the first art gallery in the city of Chicago.

Harry was the catalyst that set Baldwin Kingrey in motion. He created the store's advertising and graphics. He designed the lamps and the furnishings for the enterprise. He created the three-dimensional signage that spelled out the name of the store in two directions. But it was the commitment of Kitty and Jody that accounted for the success of the business. Their long hours, knowledge and enthusiasm for what they were selling were responsible for its positioning as a vital part of the city's retail establishment. For more than a decade, Baldwin Kingrey showcased the sculptural furniture of Alvar Aalto, Charles Eames, Bruno Mathsson and Eero Saarinen. Kitty later laughed when she recalled selling Aalto's three-legged stool for $6.25—less than the cost of the screws that held it together.

Kitty and Jody both had three children during the twelve years the store was in business. Kitty observed that, somehow, the Lord must have staggered them so that she was never out of the store for more than a week at a time. She couldn't be because Baldwin Kingrey was such a "happening" place. Architects, designers and artists mingled there and exchanged ideas. Kitty and Jody spread the good design message to the public. Young couples walking in off the street found two young working mothers who understood their needs, as well as their pocketbooks. There was an instant connection. Many of the store's furniture pieces and other housewares have become icons of high design in the last fifty years.

An Old Town Building Revolution on Willow Street

After a dozen years, Kitty sold her interest in Baldwin Kingrey in order to raise her three daughters. The Weeses joined the Lathams, the Kogans and the Ragos in the artistic hegira to Old Town and settled into a (then) revolutionary house on Willow Street. Revolutionary because it was like no other house in

The Weese row house, a revolutionary design by an extraordinary urban architect—Harry Weese. *Photo by Carolyn Blackmon.*

Old Town (until Walter Netsch built his legendary masterpiece on Hudson in 1973), and yet it fit in perfectly. Other neighborhood houses were traditional one- and two-story frame houses—some modest brick residences, a few more elaborate brick structures, some (not many) apartment buildings and a couple of truly grand old places. Harry changed that look. His houses were prototypes of what could be done on reasonable budgets, much like Kitty's own interior design selections. He designed the Willow row as private urban renewal residences: architecturally interesting, user friendly and affordable. While the façades of the houses in the row were similar, the interiors reflected the needs and tastes of their owners. The Weeses' house managed to be typically Old Town and, at the same time, typically Harry and Kitty. The small rooms comprised four distinct living areas: the first floor was for office/den/storage (much like the first-floor storage of the old balloon-frame cottages). Up a steep set of stairs was the second-floor family space—living room, dining room and kitchen (again harkening back to its Old Town roots). The third set of stairs opened onto the bedrooms. The final staircase led to Kitty's studio.

The entire house was infused with light. It was fairly small, inviting and filled with fun. Harry described it as having a "witty roof, amusing entries, improbable windows and suddenly opened spaces." Every room was a room with a view. Distinctive to the Weese house was a modular kitchen for Kitty that could be pulled out to accommodate the cook and pushed in to expand the dining space. The dining area overlooked a quintessential Old Town garden that was beautiful in all seasons of the year.

On Her Own: 1970–2005

For a number of years, Kitty looked after the Willow house and its denizens. When the Baldwin fledglings could fly on their own, Kitty also took flight. She went into interior design and did the interiors of many buildings designed by Harry—who had, by now, become internationally famous—including three floors of the Sears Tower (now the Willis Tower) and other large commercial spaces. She also designed the interior of the house on Willow Street. And, finally, she painted. She studied botanical illustration at the Botanic Gardens. She took courses in Aspen, Colorado. Eventually, she found her way to the Old Town Art Center, where she studied with renowned Illinois artist and art instructor Kay Smith until her death in 2005.

As a painter, Kitty enjoyed a period of creativity that rivaled, perhaps even surpassed, her design career. Her botanicals became sought after throughout the city. In Colorado, she had a number of one-woman shows that brought her talent and her art to a vast new audience. Even as a hot commodity in the art world, she wore her newfound fame with modesty and a sense of wonder.

It was a joy to watch Kitty create. She would spread her favorite 140-pound Arches paper on a table, lay out her colors and assemble the objects that would become the subjects of her painting. She would raise her hand, pause and then let the brush glide across the surface. The most mundane objects were transformed under that brush: a row of dancing carrots; a brilliant purple onion; two bananas pierced by a sharp wooden branch; the twin towers; a delicate green and lavender artichoke; an ugly heaven-only-knows-what that she found at the Farmers' Market and knew she had to paint; a bowl of cherries; a vase of lemons. So many subjects. So many paintings. So many magic moments.

In early 2005, while visiting in Alabama, Kitty took a debilitating fall. She was flown back to Chicago for treatment and intensive therapy. Sadly, she never recovered. She died on March 18, 2005.

She spread the white painting surface on the table before her. She assembled the various colors she would use to transform it. She arranged the items intended as the subjects of her work and took the brush between her long, graceful fingers. She held it poised above the blank surface, waiting for the moment of creativity. She lowered the brush and worked until the painting was finished. Then she signed it: Kitty.

HERMAN KOGAN, UNFORGETTABLE

In this world of over-rated pleasures, of under-rated treasures,
I'm so glad there is you.
—Jimmy Dorsey 1947

Herman Kogan was, first and foremost, a writer. He was one of the creative group who lived and worked in Old Town in the 1950s and '60s. With his wife, Marilew, and their two sons, Mark and Rick, he remained an Old Towner until the neighborhood turned from "artsy" to "yuppie" in the 1970s. There was nothing upscale or fashionable about Old Town when the Kogans arrived. It was a cultural mix of Puerto Rican, Italian, German, gypsy and just about everything else. While the neighborhood had a certain bohemian cachet, it was also rough and more than a little edgy. In Rick's words, "One had to be an urban pioneer to settle in Old Town in the '50s."

The Kogans moved into the North Park apartments (now the North Park Condominiums, but that designation was more than twenty years away) between Eugenie and St. Paul Streets. The complex had been built by Daniel Crilly as part of his Crilly Court planned community development in the late 1890s. They were exactly the kind of tenants Crilly would have wanted—a middle-class family with children connected with the arts.

Herman worked for the *Chicago Tribune*, the *Chicago Daily News* and the *Chicago Sun Times* as a reporter, critic and editor. With Lloyd Wendt (a fellow journalist and writer), he coauthored a number of books about Chicago, including biographies of notorious politicians like John "Bathhouse" Coughlin and Michael "Hinky Dink" Kenna. Perhaps their best-known collaborative effort was the history of Chicago's famous Marshall Field Department Store, *Give the*

Herman Kogan, an amazing Chicago journalist. *Photo courtesy of Rick Kogan.*

Lady What She Wants. With his son, Rick, he wrote *Yesterday's Chicago*, a pictorial history with text that provides a wonderful study of the politics, events and architecture of his city, and a history of the Walgreen Company. On his own, he wrote histories of the *Encyclopedia Britannica* and the Museum of Science and Industry. And, as a good neighbor, he wrote pieces for the Old Town Art Fair program book—most notably, in 1963, "A Quick History and Some Trivia," which began, "As you push, shove, shuffle, or stroll your way around Old Town this weekend, you may possibly want to know something of its interesting past—beyond say, the date when the first $1.50 hamburger went on sale in one of the plushier Wells Street restaurants." The article went on to recount some of Old Town's history and offer a list of a few notable residents.

As a father, Herman shared his life and his passions—literature, music, architecture and history—with his children on the assumption that those passions would somehow rub off. They did. Rick recalls that the first sound he remembers was that of his father's typewriter. In later years, the memory of that sound inspired his decision to become a writer. He also recalled that life in the Kogan household was a long series of conversations with his father, conversations of such depth and interest that school paled by comparison. It is no exaggeration to say that Herman was (and is) young Rick's hero.

Did Herman ever go out and toss a ball back and forth with his boys? Not that Rick can remember. On the other hand, he gathered the children around him while he played jazz and show tunes on the stereo (just as his friend and neighbor Dick Latham did with his children across the way on Crilly Court). Often, he would get out his violin and play along with the records—yes, the old vinyl platters—*West Side Story*, *Guys and Dolls*, *My Fair Lady*, *The Music Man*, *The Pajama Game* and *Damn Yankees*. And he shared stories with the boys about the history of Chicago and Old Town. Herman had a real sense of place and an understanding of architectural styles.

The Kogans had what Rick describes as an "artsy" household. They were the epitome of how people viewed Old Town residents in the 1950s and '60s. Herman was then the book editor and drama critic for the *Chicago Sun Times*. Marilew was the head of public relations at the Art Institute of Chicago. They were smart, literate people who gathered the great and the near great of the arts and entertainment world around them to eat, drink and talk. Folk singer Win Strake sat on the railing of their back deck, playing guitar. (The kids were beside themselves for fear he would fall off. Win was not a small man, and he was none too steady after a few drinks.) James Jones (*From Here to Eternity*, *Some Came Running*, *The Thin Red Line*) once stayed with the family for two weeks, writing one or the other of his books. Marcel Marceau, the French mime, was a frequent visitor. (Rick and Mark thought he was from outer space and were amazed when he opened his mouth to talk.) The leading satirist of the day, Mort Sahl, brought his biting political commentary and enormous wit to the parties. Actor Anthony Quinn, in town to promote what was arguably his best-known movie, *Zorba the Greek*, dropped by. Every prominent journalist in Chicago came calling. Why? Because Herman knew them, and they knew and enjoyed his company; because his was a place where they could gather, be with interesting people and relax—no hype, no agenda, no demands on their celebrity. Even Rick did not see them as famous people then. (He knows better now, although he still would not be awed.) They were just the fascinating friends of his parents, and he was the lucky kid who grew up in a household where almost every night was a party.

Herman allowed his sons the freedom to explore and make their own way around the neighborhood. Rick learned music appreciation by standing outside the clubs on Wells Street—Orphans, Mother Blues and, of course, the Earl of Old Town—nose pressed to the glass, listening to the performers.

With Herman's and Marilew's blessing, and even encouragement, Rick and Mark grew up completely comfortable and at home in their urban environment. They had no fear of their surroundings—night or day. There was a "beautiful spontaneity" about life in Old Town then. When kids could be outside, they were outside. For the most part, they did not join groups in supervised activities. If they wanted to play ball, they went out and put together a pick-up game. If they wanted to play chess, checkers or

Monopoly, they found friends who wanted to do the same thing. It was that easy. For two years running, they even organized their own Children's Art Fair (to rival the annual Old Town Art Fair) in the courtyard behind their apartment. They charged twenty-five cents admission, and they created all of the artwork—which they attached to the fences with tape. They sold every piece. The professional artists should have been so lucky.

Herman and his family left the neighborhood in 1974. They bought a house just across the Illinois state line in New Buffalo, Michigan, which Rick said was a lot like Old Town in the 1960s. In a way, they took Old Town with them. Herman and Marilew continued to host fun parties for interesting people—just a different set this time around. Those who found their way to New Buffalo included film critics Roger Ebert and Gene Siskel and political commentator Andy Shaw. By then, however, Rick and Mark were on their own. Their New Buffalo pioneering was done mainly on weekends. And it wasn't the same. How could it be?

It's different in the old apartments on North Park (now chic condominiums) today. The people who gather for parties are nameless, except to their hosts. There are no celebrities who just stop by to chat. They don't dare. Half the television stations in the city would arrive with their cameras within minutes to find out what's going on. Children do still make art in the Crilly courtyard, but now they are chalk drawings of snakes and flowers and hopscotch squares on pavement—and they vanish with the next rain. They play and ride their tricycles—under their parents' supervision—behind closed gates. And never ever do they wander along onto Wells Street to stand outside a club and listen to the music. It's no longer safe—and even if it were, there are no clubs and no music, only restaurants/bars with giant, high-density, plasma screen television sets displaying whatever sports event is going on at the moment. Times have changed.

But this is not a lament about Old Town present. It's a paean to Herman Kogan's Old Town and the world he created here in the 1950s, '60s and '70s. No matter that he physically relocated to New Buffalo; he was, and always will be, an Old Towner.

The Party's Over

So that's it, folks. The end of the greatest Old Town party ever. While it was going on, it was unrivalled: Henry Rago writing poetry, Richard Latham designing and sharing music with friends, Kitty Weese creating art and the Kogans doing it all. They are all gone now. But sometimes a whispering of leaves, a twang of guitar strings and an echo of verses on the wind brings back those days when it was all so rosy and romantic to those who were young then and who felt so intensely about their surroundings. Wasn't that a time!

Old Town Lives

The end of the 1960s was not the end of Old Town, merely the end of Old Town past. Painters still create in the artists' aeries on Weiland. A popular mystery writer creates edge-of-your-seat thrillers on Sedgwick. A gorgeous philanthropist and art patron gathers the best and brightest around her on Menomonee Street. And an Old Town terror of the court in the 1960s has become a Chicago entertainment icon and journalistic wunderkind of the early twenty-first century.

RICK KOGAN: CHICAGO BON VIVANT, BOULEVARDIER AND OLD TOWN KID

This is my kind of town, Chicago is
My kind of tow, Chicago is.
My kind of people too,
People who, smile at you.
—Sammy Kahn/Jimmy van Heusen

Rick Kogan doesn't live here anymore. He did, once. He grew up in the grand old apartment building at 1715 North Park—now the North Park Condominiums—and lived there from 1952 to 1972. He looked out over the cracked cement driveway that separated the apartments and the Crilly Court row houses—then in the throes of urban renewal. He exchanged his first teenage kiss with Mande Latham, daughter of Richard and Mary Ann Latham, who lived in one of those row houses. He joined Anthony Rago in courtyard games. He engineered and executed an art fair in which the Crilly kids displayed their paintings and neighbors walked away with every piece exhibited. He wandered Wells Street in the 1970s with his brother, Mark, standing outside the clubs and saloons with his nose pressed against the glass to get a glimpse of the stars who performed there. He made friends all over the neighborhood, and those who are still in the neighborhood remember him fondly. Now, he is the one who is the object of their awe.

His father was the legendary Herman Kogan, an editor for the *Chicago Sun Times* who immortalized the Marshall Field's motto in what was arguably his best-known work, *Give the Lady What She Wants*. Later, Rick was lucky enough to collaborate with his famous dad on *Yesterday's Chicago* and a history of the Walgreen Company.

The rest is biography. He moved away. He became famous in his own right. He wrote his first story for the *Chicago Sun Times* when he was sixteen. He helped cover the infamous Democratic Convention of 1968. He wrote about crime, entertainment and the arts. He was an investigative reporter, a feature writer and critic. He gravitated to the *Tribune* and became a TV critic and editor of the Tempo section. He created, and still hosts, *The*

Rick Kogan, like father, like son—and then some. *Photo courtesy of Rick Kogan.*

Sunday Papers on WLUP-FM radio, a show with an enormous following in and out of Chicago. He co-hosted *Media Creature* on AM 1000 radio and was a featured weekly commentator on the television program *Fox Thing in the Morning*. His latest gig is hosting *Chicago Live*, a weekly live radio show aired from the Chicago Theater and showcasing who and what is making news in Chicago, including "Almanac," a multi-media reminiscence of historic Chicago happenings in a particular year. He has authored twelve (count 'em, twelve) books, mostly about Chicago. He is a living legend of Chicago history. But all of this is, as I said, biography.

That brings us to the all-important question: just who is Rick Kogan really? He's a raconteur. Think Ring Lardner, O. Henry, Mark Twain, Will Rogers, Damon Runyon, A.J. Liebling, Garrison Keillor, John Stewart and Jay Leno all rolled into one. He's all the barbers in *Barbershop*. He's Joe the Bartender, the whole floating crap game group in *Guys and Dolls*, and Chicago's own Zorba wandering through Greek Town with his sidekick, Osgood. If Maurice Chevalier was the boulevardier of Paris, Rick Kogan is the boulevardier of the Windy City. Put him on any street, and he'll find a story to tell.

In his Sidewalks column of the *Tribune*'s *Sunday Magazine*, he chronicles the large and small places and events that constitute life in Chicago. It's funny, but when he writes about these places and events, they all become Old Town. When he wrote about the day the Magikist sign vanished from the northbound Kennedy Expressway at Montrose, that was Old Town. There was the story about the baloney makers at Drier's Meat Market in Three Oaks, Michigan, whose delectable product was an Old Town reminder. The description of Linda Lamberty—Linda who?—an unsung hero from Beverly Hills/Morgan Park and a professional genealogist who delves into neighborhood history and has worked on such projects as a Small Wonders Doll House and Miniatures Exhibit at the Ridge Historical Society was pure Old Town. His chronicle about a twenty-five-year-old mechanic named Bob Lowe, a hardworking husband whose biggest concern was providing for his family and whose life was turned upside down when he became the sole witness to a murder on Chicago's West Side in the fall of 1972—well, maybe that one is not so much Old Town as the others. But the story about an "urban idiocy" known as winter biking that involves people getting done up in Gore-Tex and riding the streets in Chicago's freezing winters, definitely smacked of some Old Town neighbors I know. Wiletta (Boo) Tatum, who owns Boo's Soul Food Café at 10936 South Vincennes Avenue and whose cooking causes regular customers like "Big Man" to go off their doctor-ordered diets with regular servings of meatloaf, mashed potatoes with gravy, green beans and (always) peach cobbler, could have come from Old Town. The developer who saved the tower of an 1850s church building in East Pilsen, long since destroyed by fire, because descendants of the founders came to him with stories, written in German, about the founding of the church had a lot of the Old Town preservationist spirit. Bill Kurtis's Kansas upbringing and his ties to the place he called home for so many years for whatever reason made me think of Old Town. The Holstein brothers, Bob Gibson, Bonnie Koloc, Kenneth Burns (Jethro of Homer and Jethro) and, well, you get the picture.

Rick Kogan doesn't live here anymore. But if he did, here are a few of the real Old Town stories he would have uncovered. He would probably have written about the night Steve Goodman sang his last chorus of "The City of New Orleans" at the Earl of Old Town. He would have written about the day Bob Meyer took the drippy rhinestone earrings off the jewelry stand and closed up shop at The Real You on Wells Street. He might have written about the time the last little retail outlets in Piper's Alley fell victim to the wrecking ball. He would have written about the demise of Paddy Bauler's DeLuxe Gardens Saloon at North Avenue and Sedgwick. He would have written about the day they swept the peanut shells out of Chances R and metamorphosed Wells Street. He would have written about the night they took last orders at the old Marge's Tavern—when Marge herself held down the bar. He might have joined the cops and hookers when they took their leave of Jeff's Laugh-In and turned out the lights. He would have watched the last feature at the old Village Theater before the projector shut down. He might even have had it his way at Burger King on LaSalle and North Avenue before it became one of the ubiquitous banks that now line the streets of Old Town.

That's what I think. But Rick Kogan doesn't live here anymore. Or does he?

11

WELLS STREET, THAT SWELL STREET

History is a pageant and not a philosophy
—Augustine Birrell

No story of Old Town would be complete without a visit to its most renowned street: Wells Street, the commercial area from Division to St. Paul that had its heyday in the 1960s and '70s and is still going strong. Before 1960, Wells Street had been a virtual slum—inhabited at the south end by poor African American families, Puerto Rican gangs and beatniks—all drawn there by low rents and lower prices. Then, almost overnight, America discovered the street, and it became a touristy, Greenwich Village–type area of Gay Nineties restaurants, hot nightclubs and smart boutiques. Prices went up. Quirky shops opened with even quirkier signs: "Sorry, We're Open," "35 Flavors of Popcorn" and "Quiet, Leathermaker at Work."

Just off Division was the House of Glunz—a wine merchant that had been in business since 1888. On Goethe, there was Mother Blues, followed by the Outhaus, the Plugged Nickel and the hungry eye. Just north was a stretch of teenybopper places where only soft drinks were sold, populated mostly by teenagers. Then there was the middle area—the so-called Phi Beta Kappa properties: Chances R, a hamburger and beer place where patrons were encouraged to throw their peanut shells on the floor; the Crystal Pistol; and Fly By Nite. Interspersed were a penny candy store and one antique shop after another. The rule of thumb for Wells Street merchants was that all of

Piper's Alley in its '70s heyday. ICHI 24998. *Photo by Henry Reichel.*

the shops had to be old, but no older than the American Revolution and no younger than World War II.

Across North Avenue was Piper's Alley, Old Town's holy grail of small shops and trendy saloons. Just inside the Alley was Charlie's General Store, the emporium of one Kris Perkins. At first glance, Charlie's appeared to be a disaster, strewn with barrels and crocks full of must-have items like back scratchers. Shelves were piled high with frying pans. Chairs and funny signs hung on the walls. "It's all planned to look as if it just sort of happened," said the genial Perkins. But like the red bandana peeking out from the pocket of his jeans, it didn't just happen. It was carefully planned.

Next to Charlie's was Penelope's Premises, a 1903-style ice cream parlor in which suburban matrons satisfied their guilty pleasures by downing ninety-five-cent ice cream sodas and a concoction known as the "$1 Integration, A Blending of Vanilla, Chocolate, and Marshmallow Without Incident." Penelope's customers could also buy anything in the place, including the tables, chairs, a brass bed and a whole collection of newly manufactured antiques. The owners had posted a sign stating that if a patron wished, s/he could buy the whole place for $275,000.

The showplace of the Alley was That Steak Joynt located at the entrance. (Note that most Wells Street establishments thought their names had to have cutsey spellings.) That Steak Joynt was, at the time, one of the most popular entertaining sites in the city. On any Saturday night, three or four chauffeur-driven Rolls-Royces followed by a fleet of Cadillacs would drive up and discharge their pleasure-seeking passengers. They came to see and be seen in the magnificent red-plush Victorian restaurant and to dine on first-rate beef dishes—$3.25 for a hamburger and up to $6.50 for a T-bone steak. The décor more than matched the food: walls covered with red velvet, six-foot-high paintings of Victorian nudes, stained-glass windows, marble statues and, over the bar, a six-hundred-pound silver light fixture that once hung over a billiard table in a British castle.

Second City cast, 1974: John Candy, Dan Aykroyd, Eugene Levy, Rosemary Radcliffe and Gilda Radner. *Second City archives.*

Second City building detail.
Photo by Carolyn Blackmon.

Next door to That Steak Joynt was the Second City, then just a little one-stage improv operation featuring comedians Joan Rivers, Alan Arkin, Avery Schreiber, John and James Belushi, Bill Murray, Dan Aykroyd and George Wendt. Today, Second City is a multiplex and international theater group occupying three floors of Piper's Alley in Chicago and performing in New York and London. Its more recent alumni include Bonnie Hunt, Jane Lynch, Steve Carell, Stephen Colbert, Tina Fey, Amy Poehler and John Lutz.

Old Town exploded with creativity in the 1960s and '70s. Big John's at 1638 North Wells Street was the hub for most of the area's musicians, painters, writers, actors, sculptors, students, photographers and models—not to mention every store owner, bartender and waitress along "the Street," as it was known in those days. Local and big-name entertainers congregated there. David Steinberg, Peter Boyle and other Second City players hung out there. Every night, University of Chicago students trekked up from Hyde Park. One evening, the manager turned away a very young-looking man who had no ID. The young man returned a few minutes later with his passport. It was Seiji Ozawa, who was conducting the Chicago Symphony Orchestra at Ravinia that summer. Ozawa became a Big John's regular whenever he was in town.

The attraction was the music—real Chicago blues. Walk through the Old Town club's squeaky doors and you could hear guitarist Mike Bloomfield and organist Barry Goldberg tear into Green Onions. Muddy Waters, Otis Spann, Nick "the Greek" Gravenites, Little Walter, Corky Siegel, Howlin' Wolf and Buddy Guy took the stage there and made Big John's one of the best blues clubs Chicago has ever known.

At 1305 North Wells was Mother Blues, a trend-setting rock club opened by a suburban housewife to fulfill a lifelong dream. Among those who appeared in her club were Peter, Paul and Mary; John Denver; Oscar Brown Jr.; Janis Joplin; George Carlin; Muddy Waters; Jefferson Airplane; and Howlin' Wolf.

OF THE EARL, STEVE GOODMAN AND WELLS STREET IN THE 1970s

It Was the Best of Times

Of all the happening places on Wells Street in that era, none was quite like the Earl of Old Town, owned and operated by Earl J.J. Pionke—known simply as "the Earl." The club is legendary among entertainers and audiences alike. No one who went there will ever forget being part of that scene. And those who weren't fortunate enough to crowd in and listen to Bonnie Koloc, Kris Kristoferson, John Prine, the Holstein brothers or Steve Goodman speak longingly of what they missed. While everyone, present or not, knows some things about the Earl of Old Town, there is still a hidden aspect to its history. And a fascinating story to tell.

THAT COZY LITTLE NIGHTCLUB ON WELLS STREET

When Earl Pionke first decided to open a pub, he said he just wanted to have fun. Earl had always tried to have fun, from the time he was one of fifteen kids living in a foster home on the south side. He learned how to hustle early and even started earning a living when he was seven by delivering newspapers. He bragged that he delivered more papers than any fifty other kids. On his route, he would sell raffle tickets to drawings for five cents and pocket half of the take. After he had sold one hundred tickets, he got a free pass to the Crane Theater, where he would watch three cowboy features at a stretch.

When he was twelve, Earl moved to the North Side. He presented himself at St. Michael's Catholic Grammar School and declared that he was ready to be saved. The salvation of his soul was not Earl's primary motive for enrolling in the school, however. By his own admission, he wasn't really interested in the "saving stuff." The school served free soft drinks and sandwiches, and the boy was hungry.

At the age of thirteen, he started a little business to support his mother and sisters. He converted a buggy into a rolling hot dog stand and undersold the regular hot dog vendors. They sold their dogs for twenty cents. Earl sold his for fifteen cents and gave three slices of tomato instead of one. He annihilated the competition.

At Waller High School, Earl made the basketball team. Members got free tickets to the old Chicago Stags pro basketball games. Earl and his friends gathered up tickets other team players weren't going to use and sold them for $1 each in front of the stadium. He made $5 or $6 at every game. When he graduated from Waller in 1950, Earl worked at a lot of jobs but ended up tending bar at Pier Nine, a saloon on North and Halsted. He ran the place for several years. After work, he would go over to the Old Towne Ale House on North Avenue for a beer. He noticed that the owner always had classical music playing at the bar, which attracted artists and writers to the yet undiscovered Old Town. Ever one with an eye for business, Earl saw that the owner was making money with the music concept, so he decided to do something similar. He began looking around for a place of his own and found it in a going-out-of-business antique shop on North and Wells. He persuaded a couple of his friends to go in with him and leased the building. The landlord was asking $150 a month. Earl sensed that the area was about to explode, and that meant rent increases. So he cut a deal with the landlord: he would pay $300 a month to start with a two-year lease and two (three-year) options at no increase in rent. The landlord was quick to take the deal. He figured he couldn't lose. He was wrong.

Earl and his partners worked through the winter of '61 converting the store into a bar. When they finally opened, nothing happened. People went in only when they couldn't get into the enormously popular Chances R or one of the other hot clubs. Even though Earl acted as bartender, porter, cook and waiter, he barely broke even. He also experimented with all kinds of entertainment, but nothing clicked. In the meantime, Earl bought out his partners and soldiered on. Good luck finally came his way. Mother Blues went out of business, and Earl took over folk music as his signature entertainment feature. It was a winner.

At first, performers found the Earl to be a tough place to work because of a bad sound system and an often-rowdy clientele. When Earl improved the sound and hired a manager to kick out the rowdies, the talent came, and so did the customers. One of his best performers, John Prine, even named an album to honor the place, *Gathering at the Earl of Old Town*.

MEET ME AT THE EARL

If you wandered into the Earl on any given evening, the first person you would see was the man himself tending bar. Earl was a tall man with a bar fighter's build, hip hair, a scruffy goatee and the beginning of a gut. Behind the cash register, you'd find Pete the Bartender. Another bartender would be washing glasses and drawing beer. Jimmy Johnson—"Ptomaine Jim"—would be presiding at the grill, and manager Gus Johns would be guarding the door. There might be a couple of folk singers hanging out and a few regulars waiting to hear the music, live on stage seven nights a week.

The first person responsible for bringing in a crowd was Bonnie Koloc, an extraordinary folk singer. Though she had achieved national fame by this time, she kept coming back to the Earl—sometimes because she was broke, but mostly because of Earl himself. They had a great relationship. He could say almost anything to her, and she would take it in the good-natured way it was intended. One day, for example, she walked in, beautiful as ever, but looking definitely dowdy. "Where in the hell did you get that dress?" asked Earl.

"What do you think of it?" Koloc answered. "I got it at a secondhand store."

Earl grinned and said nothing.

Although Earl took a paternal interest in most of his performers, one of his favorites was Steve Goodman. Earl had a little place in back of the club where singers went to hang out and play a puck bowling game between sets. He called it "the Sneak Joynt." It was a frame house and looked as though General Grant might have slept there—or drunk there, at the very least. Once, when Goodman and Earl had engaged in a name-calling argument, the singer stalked out to the "Joynt," cursing. When Earl confronted Steve about the problem, he confessed that he wasn't happy with his new album and said he thought he was overexposed in Chicago. "Listen, you SOB,"

Earl shouted, "it's a very good album. But that doesn't make any difference. An album is nothing. You're an entertainer. You could sing in my place for years!" Goodman wasn't convinced.

Later that same evening, Bonnie Koloc finished her act to wild applause and performed two encores. The audience kept yelling and stomping for more. Earl went back through the crowd to his office and called Steve in the back room. "Listen, you bleep. It's too bad you don't want to work anymore—especially in Chicago where you're overexposed—'cause I got an audience out here that just won't quit."

Goodman was onstage in five minutes. Backed up by Koloc's band, he launched into "The City of New Orleans" followed by "The Lincoln Park Towing Company." Then he sang the numbers he did best—hillbilly songs. Halfway through his rendition of a Hank Williams tune, a conventioneer from Tulsa called his buddies back at the Drake Hotel. "I told you we would find the jumpingest place in town," he shouted. Then he held out the phone so they could hear what they were missing.

Back at the bar, Earl was grinning.

THE STORY OF A CHICAGO HOMEBOY—STEVE GOODMAN

Go, Cubs go,
Go, Cubs go.
Hey Chicago, what do you say
The Cubs are gonna' win today.
—*Steve Goodman*

For those of you who have never heard of or don't know much about Steve Goodman, here is a part of his story. In addition to being one awesome folk singer and composer, he wrote what has become the anthem for almost everyone who lives on the north side of Chicago. Win or lose, they all love to sing "Go, Cubs Go," whether at the game, on the sidewalks outside Wrigley Field or in any one of the bars around their beloved park.

Steve Goodman was born and raised in Chicago. He began writing and performing songs as a teenager. In 1969, after a brief stay in New York, he came back to Chicago and became a regular at the Earl of Old Town on Wells Street, as well as other well-known clubs in the city. I saw him at the

Earl in the late 1970s and liked his singing so much that I went up to him after one set and asked to buy him a drink. "Blackberry wine," he said. Not surprisingly, Earl had a bottle—no doubt just for him—blackberry wine hardly being the drink of choice among the club's patrons.

In 1971, Goodman was performing at both the Earl and a bar called the Quiet Knight, where he was the opening act for Kris Kristofferson. Kristofferson was so impressed with the young folk singer that he promptly introduced him to Paul Anka. Anka was blown away. He flew Goodman to New York to record some demos. One night, while in New York, Goodman met folk singer Arlo Guthrie in a bar and persuaded him to listen to one of his songs. It wasn't easy. Guthrie hated being asked to listen to an unknown's demos, and he hated being confronted on his own time. Finally, however, he agreed, but only if Goodman would buy him a beer. That beer was the best investment Steve Goodman ever made. Guthrie liked the song so much that he asked to record it, and his version of the song brought in enough money to enable Steve to make music his full-time career. After Guthrie, Johnny Cash, Judy Collins and Willie Nelson all recorded the song, which was none other than "The City of New Orleans." Kristofferson pronounced it "the best damn train song ever written":

> *Good morning America, how are you?*
> *Don't you know me, I'm your native son.*
> *I'm the train they call The City of New Orleans,*
> *I'll be gone five hundred miles when the day is done.*

THE ULTIMATE OLD TOWN AND CUBS FAN

No matter where he went, Steve Goodman was, at heart, a Chicagoan—in the same way Jim Belushi and Joe Mantegna are today. He wrote and performed many songs about the city, including "The Lincoln Park Pirates," about the notorious Lincoln Park Towing Company, and "Daley's Gone," a tribute to the late mayor Richard J. Daley. But his best-known Chicago songs were about his beloved Cubs.

Cubs fans are a different breed. They're loyal, they're rowdy and they're embarrassingly optimistic. No matter what kind of season the team starts out having, they usually end up losing—hence the nickname, the "Loveable Losers." The mantra of every Cub fan is "Wait till next year." The first of

Steve Goodman's Cubs songs was called "A Dying Cub Fan's Last Request," and it is still played at the start of every baseball season in Chicago. It was introduced on Roy Leonard's WGN radio show in 1981. Steve walked into the studio with Jethro Burns and told Roy that he had played a new song at the Park West club the night before and that he would like to perform it on Leonard's show. Leonard agreed, and with Jethro on banjo, Steve picked up his guitar and started to sing:

By the shores of old Lake Michigan
Where the hawk wind blows so cold,
An old Cub fan lay dying
In his midnight hour that tolled.
Round his bed his friends had all gathered,
They knew his time was short.
He told them, "It's late, and it's getting dark in here,
And I know it's time to go.
But before I leave the line-up,
There's just one thing I'd like to know,
Do they still play the blues in Chicago
When the baseball season rolls around.
When the snow melts away,
Do the Cubbies still play
In their ivy-covered burial ground?
When I was a boy, they were my pride and joy.
But now, they only bring fatigue
To the home of the brave,
The land of the free,
And the doormat of the National League."

A lot of people thought the song was autobiographical because Goodman was battling leukemia. The disease would claim his life just three years later. Although the lyrics sound downbeat, they are really Steve's affectionate, albeit bluesy, salute to the perpetual failure at Wrigley Field. After all, he had cut his musical teeth on the Chicago blues in Wells Street pubs.

The song put him on bad paper with the Cubs front office, which in 1981 was trying to shake the "Loveable Loser" image. The general manager, Dallas Green, hated the song and declared that Steve Goodman was no fan of the Cubs. He was wrong.

Three years later, at the height of what promised to be a good season, WGN commissioned Steve to write a more upbeat song about the Cubs. That song turned out to be "Go, Cubs Go." The team and the WGN executives loved the song so much that they asked Steve to record it, which he did, along with Cubs players Thad Bosley, Jay Johnstone, Jody Davis, Gary Matthews and Keith Moreland. It was an instant hit and sold more than seventy-four thousand copies—more than any other album or song Steve Goodman had ever recorded. Ironically, Goodman wrote the song about the time he learned that the experimental leukemia treatments he had undergone did not work. He was dying.

The Cubs went on a winning streak that season, and it became clear they were going to make it to the playoffs. They asked Steve to sing the national anthem at the first playoff game. He was thrilled to accept. He didn't make it. He died four days before the Cubs clinched the National League East Division title with a victory over the Pittsburgh Pirates. His good friend Jimmy Buffet sang the anthem for him.

At one point, Steve had jokingly said that when he died, he wanted to be cremated and have his ashes scattered over home plate at Wrigley Field so they would blow out and find their final resting place on Waveland Avenue. His partner, Al Bunetta, asked Cubs management for permission to do this, pointing out that Steve was such a devoted Cubs fan and that he had written two songs that would forever be part of Cubs lore. The team officials refused.

Three years went by. Finally, Steve's brother, Dave, took matters into his own hands. He spoke to someone who knew someone who would let him in. Just before opening day in 1988, a group of Steve's friends went up into the bleachers and scattered a portion of his ashes out over left field. (His widow and daughters scattered the remainder over home plate at Doubleday Field in Cooperstown, New York.) Now, whenever the Cubs win and fans start to sing "Go, Cubs Go," a part of Steve Goodman—and quite possibly a part of Earl J.J. Pionke and the old gang from the Earl—will be listening.

12

THE HAUNTING

The past remains integral to us all, individually and collectively. We must concede the ancients their place...but their place is not simply back there in a separate foreign country; it is assimilated in ourselves, and resurrected into an ever-changing present.
—*David Lowenthal*

It seems fitting that we should end our Old Town hidden history odyssey on Menomonee Street at its most recognizable landmark: the little yellow house on the corner. History tours stop here. Architectural tours stop here. Bicycle tours stop here. Even World Wide Food Tours stop here. And so will we.

BEHIND EVERY GREAT HOUSE—A HIDDEN STORY

There is a lot of history on the corner of Menomonee and North Park in Old Town. Much of it is to be found in two buildings, the visible yellow house at number 314 and the almost hidden house in back. The back house has always been obscured by the larger buildings to the east and west, but it has sat with simple dignity on a plot of land just off the sidewalk. Few people know it, but the tiniest cathedral in the world was located in that little house. It was built in 1932, and even then, the only decoration and the only indication that this was a place of worship was a cross, high atop its front gable. That cross identified the little building as the Assyrian Church of the East.

The tiniest cathedral in the world, in back of the yellow house on Menomonee Street. *Photo by Steve Weiss.*

Who are the Assyrians? They are the indigenous people of Mesopotamia and have a history spanning over sixty-seven hundred years. Assyrian civilization at one time incorporated the entire Near East, most notably the area of the Fertile Crescent. The heartland (Northern Mesopotamia) of Assyria lies in present-day northern Iraq, southeastern Turkey, northeastern Syria and northwestern Iran. The remains of its ancient capital, Nineveh, are in northern Iraq.

The first Assyrians who came to Chicago in the 1880s were seminarians. They were followed by medical students in the 1890s. Like many other émigrés, they came to escape the persecution inflicted on them by the non-Christian rulers in the countries where they resided. By the turn of the century, about thirty Assyrian families and six hundred young men migrated to Chicago. The number grew to three thousand in the 1920s, with the greatest concentration around Clark and Huron Streets.

By the 1930s, many in the Assyrian community moved north to Lincoln Park, Lakeview and Uptown. More arrived from Iran, Iraq and Syria through the 1940s, until, in 1944, there were approximately five thousand Assyrians living in the Chicago—the largest number in any American city. This number continued to increase throughout the twentieth century as Assyrians fled persecution and the hardships of war in their home countries.

The Church of the East, one of the oldest Christian churches, was established in the first century AD. It follows the Julian calendar and takes its doctrine from the Nicene Creed. Spiritual jurisdiction is vested in a patriarch. At the time of the establishment of the Old Town Church of the East, the leader of the Assyrian Church of the East worldwide was patriarch His Beatitude Mar Eshai Shimum XXIII, Catholicos CXIX, who lived on Sheridan Road. The patriarchate, whose succession descends from uncle to nephew, was held by the Shimum family for more than seven hundred years. Shimum was assassinated by an estranged relative in 1975, and in 1976, Mar Dinkha IV, Metropolitan of Tehran until the Iran-Iraq War of 1980–88, was named his successor.

Assyrian members of the Chicago parish held services in the St. James Episcopal Chapel until 1932. While this was adequate, the worshippers really wanted a place of their own. The congregation of about two hundred members organized and built the "tiniest" cathedral with their own hands. They held services every Sunday morning, usually led by the Reverend Isaac Rehana, who came to Chicago from Cyprus. The sermon was given in modern Assyrian, but the rest of the service was conducted in Aramaic. In addition to Sunday services, the Old Town congregation had a youth organization and a ladies' group called Daughters of the Church. Eventually, however, the little church could not sustain itself, and its members gravitated to the larger community of Christian Arabs living on the northwest side.

The tiny cathedral and its grounds were vacant until 2010, when the owner of the property at 314 West Menomonee decided to buy it and convert it to a guesthouse. True to the Old Town tradition, he kept many of the building's historical features. It is still partially hidden by its larger neighbors. And the faithful who follow the little stone path to the front door are not worshippers. They are friends, neighbors and tourists who want to mingle with one another and with a bit of history.

THE GHOSTS OF OLD TOWN: ANOTHER HIDDEN STORY

Oh, no one knows what goes on behind closed doors.
—Charlie Rich

If you believe what some tour guides say about Old Town, almost every house was either haunted or a domicile for "ladies of the evening." Maybe, and maybe not. Yes, there were at least two verifiable bordellos on Crilly Court in the 1920s and '30s (see chapter 8). And we have accounts of two haunted sites in the neighborhood—not verifiable, but not disproved either.

THE PHANTOMS OF THE STEAK JOYNT

Legend has it that the now-vanished Steak Joynt restaurant at the entrance of Piper's Alley on Wells Street was once one of the city's most haunted locations. Among its haunted features was a marble bust of a grinning peasant with a wine flask in his hands in the center of the main-floor dining room. The bust was a relic from the now-defunct Matson Steamship Line. Over the years, it gained an unusual reputation. It was said that if you looked at the peasant's face long enough, his expression would change. Some attributed unique powers to the bust. A stockbroker swore that the statue gave him useful stock tips. Others were certain that it had cured a variety of their ailments. With all this talk, paranormal investigations of the building were undertaken. During one of these investigations, a photograph was taken of the bust using special infrared film. The negative showed two white fingers of energy, seemingly generated by the marble peasant. While the expression change, healing powers and stock tips can easily be explained away, the photograph remains unexplained.

There were other unexplained Steak Joynt "oddities." On the walls of the staircase leading to the upper-floor dining room were portraits of William and Catherine Devine. Soon after the portrait of Catherine was hung, customers spoke of feeling a cold gust on the stairs between the paintings. Others said that if they looked at Catherine's face in the opposite mirror, she could be seen smiling—but when they looked at the painting directly, the smile vanished. They also had the feeling that Catherine's eyes were following them as they ascended the stairs. The ghost stories became so

That Steak Joynt, a popular Chicago restaurant and nightclub said to be haunted. ICHI 26328. *Photo by Henry Reichel.*

widespread that in the 1980s, the owners of the establishment decided to test their veracity. They brought in a local medium, Robert Dubell, to conduct the séances. During one session, Dubell and others revealed that they had made contact with three spirits who were haunting the place. One identified himself as the architect who had designed the building; the second claimed she was a female customer from the original Piper's Bakery; and the third would not reveal his identity. Speculation had it that he was a murder victim who had some connection with the building in the nineteenth century. The séance that night was attended by a *Sun Times* reporter who, strangely, became violently ill during the session.

Not surprisingly, it became difficult to get employees who would come in and work in the restaurant after hours, especially janitors and cleaning ladies. No one wanted to be there when the restaurant was closed, especially after stories circulated of singing sounds and the appearance of apparitions. One janitor became so frightened by what he thought he saw one evening that he ran out screaming—leaving the door unlocked and his paycheck uncollected. He never went back. Waiters reported having spotted shadowy figures on many occasions. In 1991, a staff member who was locking the front door felt a hand gripping his shoulder and pulling him backward. When he turned around, no one was there. Some women who went into the restrooms claimed to have heard the hard-soled shoes of people coming in behind them—only to find that they were the sole occupants. One waitress, who was clearing tables in the upstairs lounge area, was grabbed and roughly dragged across the floor. When she screamed, some staff ran up the stairs to see what happened. They found the server on the floor with the heel of her shoe broken off and red welts on her arm. There was no assailant.

On two occasions, in 1991 and 1994, the owners invited members of Chicago's Ghost Research Society and some media people to spend the night in the place and to record what they witnessed. In the 1991 visit, the restaurant was divided into sections, each watched over by investigators with cameras, tape recorders and other electronic devices. The photographs yielded some interesting results—including a glowing red light; a white, crescent-shaped light near the women's restroom; and a monk-like figure hovering over a table in what appeared to be a robe. His upper torso and lower extremities were intact, but the middle portion of his body was missing.

A similar group congregated in 1994. One gentleman reported seeing the door to the kitchen opening on its own. He reported feeling a cold draft when he went near the area to check out the cause. In addition, he noted that the door had opened against the draft. This meant that it had to have been pushed open, which was bizarre because no one attending the gathering was physically in the space. The second group of investigators also reported flickering lights, cold spots, phantom footsteps, the sound of someone being dragged across the upstairs floor and a figure without a middle sitting over a downstairs dining table. All of this remains unexplained, which makes one wonder if Old Town really is haunted. And this leads to another paranormal phenomenon: the ghost in the yellow house on Menomonee.

A Haunting in a Historic Menomonee House

The house at 314 West Menomonee hasn't always been so yellow. It has evolved from burned-out charcoal to dull brown, to deep red, to pale lemon, to gray, to its present corncake yellow. The first house on the site appears to have been constructed in 1869 by a Mr. Eben F. Runyan. That house burned to the ground in the Great Fire of 1871. The deed to the property passed to John Waldo in 1876. Mr. Waldo built a "kit" house on the lot using lumber that had been collected from the fire. Since the date of construction is given as 1876, it is likely that the house was built without a permit, frame

Old Town's most recognizable house, the yellow house on Menomonee. *Photo courtesy of Steve Weiss.*

construction having been banned within the city limits after 1874. Mr. Waldo bought the framing, the clapboards and the felt lining for the inside walls in one package and constructed the house himself. The current owner says that, on days when the wind is right, he can stand outside the building and detect the scent of burnt wood. Imagine, a lingering scent that had its origins in 1871!

The original cottage was nineteen by twenty-two feet. It has been enlarged twice over the years. It is likely that the house also had an attached stable. In all probability, horses were pastured in what is now the driveway and housed in the stable. Since there are carriage houses across the street, it is logical to assume that the horses had to go somewhere, and this driveway was one of the few spots that never had a building on it.

Mr. Waldo died in 1898. Mrs. Waldo remained in the house for ten more years. After that, it changed owners every few years. As for the bordello rumor—it is just that, a rumor. There is nothing in the records to show that the property was ever anything but a conventional residence: single family, two family and back to single family. The colorful past was in paint only.

A distinctive feature of the property is its garden—especially its old door with just enough character and dilapidation to be interesting. Passersby often ask to be photographed next to this door. Some send the photos back to relatives and friends as mementos. When the owners first talked about what kind of door they wanted on the space, they came up with the idea that it should look like a door leading to a secret garden, following the well-known children's story. They searched until they found one with just the right age and sense of magic.

The yellow house is famous for the lights that overhang the driveway and change with the seasons: red for Valentine's Day, green for St. Patrick's Day, burnt orange for fall and blue for winter. When the family looks out their upstairs windows, they can see cars and pedestrians slow down to look at the lights.

Halloween lives up to the magic promise of the old gate. The yard is filled with goblins and witches. Spider webs crisscross the area. A fog machine creates thick mist, and screams erupt from outdoor speakers. Early in the evening, trick-or-treaters stop to fill their treat bags. When they leave, the adults take over to cook hot dogs, toast marshmallows and tell ghost stories. The whole neighborhood is welcomed, and it is one of the truest examples of community spirit that can be found in the city.

THE EXTRAORDINARY WEISS FAMILY: THE OLD TOWN BEAT GOES ON

The residents inside the yellow house are as colorful as its façade. They embody the essence of Old Town ingenuity and creativity. Steve Weiss, the patriarch, is an internationally known filmmaker and leader in the indie film community. He is also a film/video entrepreneur with over five hundred productions to his credit. He has been piling up awards from film festivals all over the country, including the Houston, Chicago and New York Film Festivals. He began his career videotaping weddings and has gone on to build a video empire that includes Zacuto Rentals and Zacuto

Steve Weiss, master of the haunted house. *Photo courtesy of Steve Weiss.*

USA (Zacuto is the name of Steve's grandfather). Zacuto has a product line of over 140 items, making Steve one of the leading trendsetters in camera package design. He is the director of *FilmFellas* and *Critics*, two webisodic series. His 2010 web series *The Great Camera Shootout* won an Emmy for best informational program.

Steve's wife, Lucy, is also multitalented. She paints and is an expert gardener who has won prizes for her gardening layout and design. Every year, she walks away with first prize in a local cooking contest (one neighbor says she's secretly writing a cookbook featuring these recipes). She is also a singular beauty, the subject of Steve's series of 1950s-style noir movie photographs that bring to mind a young Garbo.

Daughter Isabel proves that the branch doesn't fall far from the tree. She is a young artist prodigy who is the envy of painters several times her age. She once created over one hundred original paintings to send as invitations to one of her parents' garden parties. She is also a photographer who has been taking pictures since she was two. Yet with all this talent, she is not some genius child wrapped in a cocoon. She is simply an extraordinarily gifted little lady who loves to sing, dance and play while chattering away endlessly in English and Polish. (She is completely bilingual.)

The Haunting

Right: Lucy Weiss. She hears dead people. *Photo courtesy of Steve Weiss*.

Below: Isabel Weiss, pixie in the house. *Photo courtesy of Steve Weiss*.

And now—the promised hidden story of the Menomonee Street ghost. Sometimes, when Steve is away and Lucy stands in her upstairs hallway, she can hear a sad voice calling, "LUCEE, LUCEE." She does not recognize the caller, but she has a theory about who it might be.

In 1857, Charles H. Kees was born. One year later, Lucy Sophia Rossman was born. Charles and Lucy met years later and were married in 1890. They had two children: Mildred, born in 1901, and Newel, born in 1907. The family moved to the little house on Menomonee in 1918, during the First World War. They lived there happily until 1932, when Charles Kees passed away. Lucy left the house after her husband's death, not realizing that he would come back to search for her. But this is Old Town, after all, and strange things happen here. The current Lucy believes that the voice calling plaintively out of the shadowy darkness is that of Charles Kees. He has come back to look for his Lucy, not realizing that she has moved on. He is trying to reconnect with her in the house where they lived as a family. Lucy Weiss can't prove this, of course. But no one can disprove it either. Until they do, that's her story, and she's sticking to it.

THE JOURNEY ENDS

We proceed out of history into history again.
—Sidney Alexander

We'll meet again,
Don't know where, don't know when,
But I know we'll meet again some sunny day.
—Ross Parker/Hughie Charles

We have reached the end of our Old Town Magical History Tour. During the journey, you have experienced the hidden story of a neighborhood—old, new and always changing. You have lived the excitement of children on the best of their school days. You have sat around the warmth of neighbors' fireplaces and listened to their music. You have looked through storefront windows and felt the wonder of what was happening inside. You have played catch in a courtyard, listened to the stories of an Arctic adventurer, pounded gold with a young man trying to find his place in the world and sat through séances where otherworldly creatures joined those of this time and place in a macabre pas de deux.

The Haunting

A typical Old Town street: nineteenth-century houses in the shadow of St. Michael's. *Oil painting by Norman Baugher*.

Time now to hit save, click the escape key and close the computer. I have finished this story. But there will be another.

All my life I shall remember knowing you, all the pleasures I have found
* in showing you*
The different ways that one may face the changing light and changing shade,
Happiness that must die, melodies that must fly,
Memories that must fade—dusty and forgotten bye and bye.
I'll see you again, whenever spring breaks through again.
Time may lie heavy between, but what has been is past forgetting.
This sweet memory across the years will come to me,
Though my world may go awry, in my heart will ever lie
Just the echo of a sigh, goodbye.

—Noel Coward

BIBLIOGRAPHY

Abbott, Karen. *Sin in the Second City*. New York: Random House, 2007.

Appelbaum, Stanley. *The Chicago World's Fair of 1893: A Photographic Record*. New York: Dover Publications, Inc., 1980.

Bach, Ira J., and Susan Wolfson. *Chicago on Foot*. Chicago: Chicago Review Press, 1994.

Baugher, Shirley. A*t Home in Our Old Town: Every House Has a Story*. Chicago: Old Town Triangle Association, 2005.

————. *Our Old Town: The History of a Neighborhood*. Chicago: Old Town Triangle Association, 2001.

Bernstein, Arnie. *Hollywood on Lake Michigan*. Chicago: Lake Claremont Press, 1998.

Brunetti, John. *Baldwin Kingrey: Midcentury Modern in Chicago*. Chicago: Wright, 2004.

Bullough, Vern L., ed. *Before Stonewall*. New York: Harrington Park Press, 2002.

Cromie, Robert. *The Great Chicago Fire*. New York: Rutledge Hill Press, 1958. Reprint, 1994.

Cronin, William. *Nature's Metropolis: Chicago and the Great West*. New York: W.W. Norton & Company, 1991.

Drell, Adrienne, ed. *20th Century Chicago: 100 Years*. Champaign, IL: 100 Voices Sports Publishing, Inc., 2000.

Drury, John. *Old Chicago Houses*. Chicago: University of Chicago Press, 1941. Reprint, 1975.

Grossman, James R., Ann Durkin Keating and Janice L. Reiff. *The Encyclopedia of Chicago*. Chicago: Newberry Library with the cooperation of the Chicago Historical Society, 2004.

Harris, Cyril M., ed. *Illustrated Dictionary of Historic Architecture*. New York: Dover Publications, Inc., 1977.

Hibbard, Angus. *Hello Goodbye: My Story of Telephone Pioneering*. Chicago: A.C. McClurg & Co. Publishers, 1941.

Hucke, Matt, and Ursula Bielski. *Graveyards of Chicago*. Chicago: Lake Claremont Press, 1999.

Keating, Ann Durkin, ed. *Chicago Neighborhoods and Suburbs: A Historical Guide*. Chicago: University of Chicago Press, 2008.

Kogan, Herman, and Rick Kogan. *Yesterday's Chicago*. Miami, FL: E.A. Seemann Publishing, Inc., 1976.

Liebling, A.J. *Chicago: The Second City*. New York: Alfred A. Knopf, 1952.

McNulty, Elizabeth. *Chicago: Then & Now*. San Diego, CA: Thunder Bay Press, 2000.

Morris, Robert R. *St. Michael's Parish: Chicago's Old Town Legend*. Chicago: St. Michael's Parish, 2003.

Sawyers, June Skinner. *Chicago Portraits*. Chicago: Loyola University Press, 1991.

Sinkevitch, Alice, ed. *AIA Guide to Chicago*. New York: Harcourt Brace & Company, 1993.

Spinney, Robert G. *City of Big Shoulders*. Chicago: Northern Illinois University Press, 2000.

Watt, David, and Leslie Watt, eds. *1871 Old Town*. Chicago: Triangle Association, 1971.

Articles

Baugher, Shirley. "The Boys of October." *Old Town Times*, October 2007.

———. "What a Long Strange Trip It's Been." *Justice for Women, Law in American Society Journal for the National Center for Law-Focused Education* 3, no. 3 (n.d.).

Bell, J.L. "David Kennison." Not Credible Blog, December 19, 2010.

Bridges, Les. "The Earl Is Just Folks." *Chicago Tribune*, April 29, 1973.

Burrows, Sara. "City Awash in Brewing History." *Pioneer Press Skyline*, April 14, 2005.

Chicago Gay and Lesbian Hall of Fame. "Henry Gerber Inducted." 1992 (posthumous).

Church of the Three Crosses. "Celebrating Our Heritage." N.d.

Chrystal, William G. "German Congregationalism on the American Frontier." Evangelical and Reformed Church, UCC, Adamstown, Maryland.

Feinberg, Leslie. "German Movement Inspired U.S. Organizing." *Workers World*, 2005.

Forkert, L.D.S. "The Old Burial Ground." *Old Town Art Fair Program Book*, 1953.

Gerber, Henry. "Hitlerism and Homosexuality." *OutHistory*, September 1934.

———. "I Wanted to Help Solve the Problem." *OutHistory*, 1920–25.

Gill, Donna. "Chicago's Old Town Tourist Attraction." *Chicago Tribune*, December 3, 1967.

Gold Leaf Factory International Pty., Ltd. "The Art of Gilding, The Power of Gold." N.d.

Goldstein, Seymour, and Doe Goldstein. "Old Town Architecture." *Old Town Art Fair Program Book*, 1965.

Gonzalez, Diane. "The Old Town Triangle Historic District." *Lincoln Parker*, Summer 1997.

Hill, Lee. "History of Old Town Through the Headlines." Paper Presented at Old Town Triangle, January 18, 1990.

Historic American Buildings Survey. "Ann Halsted Townhouses." Office of Archeology and Historic Preservation, National Park Service Department of the Interior, n.d.

Holabird, John A., Jr. "Old Town Architecture." *Old Town Art Fair Program Book*, 1964.

Hunt, Ridgely. "Savoring Wells Street." *Chicago Tribune*, June 7, 1964.

Joseph, Richard. "A Travel Columnist Discovers Our Town." *Chicago Tribune*, May 26, 1968.

Kogan, Herman. "A Sense of History, More or Less." *Old Town Art Fair Program Book*, 1959.

Kristak, Simon. "The New Old Town: Clinging to a Historic Past." *Echo*, 1997.

Kufrin, Joan. "I Remember Wells Street." *Chicago Daily News*, October 17, 1964.

Lewis, Dr. Charles Josiah. "The Strange Case of David Kennison." *Oak Park Oak Leaves*, 1914.

Lister, Walter, Jr. "1851 and All That…or the Birth and Christening of Old Town." *Old Town Art Fair Program Book*, 1960.

Moffett, Nancy. "Work Brings New Life to Old Town Parsonage." *Chicago Sun Times*, July 1, 2001.

New York Times. "Stonewall Rebellion." April 10, 2009.

Olin, Linda. "Bensinger Crilly Court: An Experience in City Living." Unpublished thesis, April 1980.

Parsons, Paul. "How to Make a Wood Stove Board." eHow. http://www.ehow.com/how_5017445_make-wood-stove-board.html.

Renowned Old Town Group. "Paddy Bauler: Alderman, Saloon Keeper, Pretend Irish, Big Fat Guy." Part 1, April 21, 2010; Part 2, May 11, 2010. Renown Old Town Blog Site. http://renownoldtown.blogspot.com.

Rosenthal, Phil, and John Hall. "We're Going to Become Stronger. My Take: John Hall CEO Goose Island Beer." *Chicago Tribune*, April 3, 2011.

Searching, Godfrey. "Political Reporting, The Way It Was." *Christian Science Monitor*, October 29, 2002.

Spink, George. "Blues for Big Johns." Jazz Institute of Chicago, n.d.

Watt, David. "1966 and All That." *Old Town Triangle Program Book*, 1966.

Weissenborn, Leo. "Her Is Old Town Past." *Old Town Art Fair Program Book*, 1955.

———. "Old Town in Retrospect." Unpublished memoir, 1955.

Wikipedia, s.v. "Society for Human Rights." http://en.wikipedia.org/wiki/Society_for_Human_Rights.

Wilson, Leslie Perrin. "A Favorite Concord Winter Sport: Moving Houses." *Concord Journal*, n.d.

Young, Cassie. "Recognizing Prominence: A Creative Look at the Lives of Henry Gerber, Richard Grune and Marsha P. Johnson." THEA 209, Final Paper.

INDEX

About the Author

S hirley Baugher has been an Old Towner for more than thirty years. She came to the community in 1978. It was only to be a temporary move—a place for her husband to hang out while she went to the Cordon Bleu in Paris to learn to become a professional chef. She hung up her toque a long time ago, and she is still in Old Town.

Through the years, Shirley has served her adopted neighborhood as a volunteer for the various programs and activities of the Old Town Triangle Association and was president of that organization for three years. She wrote three books about Old Town, describing its history, its architecture and its famous (and near-famous) inhabitants. In 2006, she won a Landmarks Preservation award for her history of Old Town. In 2011, she was recognized by Mayor Richard M. Daley as one of Chicago's outstanding women during Women's History Month.

Shirley came to Old Town from Evanston, a city almost as familiar to her as Old Town. She is a fixture at Northwestern University, where she earned her three degrees: bachelor of science in speech, master of arts in history and doctor of philosophy. She happily declares to anyone who will listen that famed composer Dimitri Shostakovich placed her PhD in her hands and gave the commencement address (in Russian). She was ecstatic. Her parents were proud but befuddled.

Shirley touts Old Town to audiences far and wide. She helps schoolchildren understand the history and significance of the special area in which they are being educated. She conducts seminars at the Chicago History Museum for those who wish to act as docents and conduct tours throughout historic Old Town. And she frequently opens her 1885 row house to tour groups who wish to see the original features and interior layout of a home listed on the National Register of Historic Places.

She has been married to her husband, Norman, for forty years and is the proud parent of one son, Scott, and an awesome grandson, Alex.